The Measurement Nightmare

How the Theory of Constraints Can Resolve Conflicting Strategies, Policies, and Measures

The St. Lucie Press/APICS Series on Constraints Management

Series Advisors

Dr. James F. Cox, III
University of Georgia
Athens, Georgia

Thomas B. McMullen, Jr.
McMullen Associates
Weston, Massachusetts

Titles in the Series

The Measurement Nightmare

How the Theory of Constraints Can Resolve Conflicting Strategies, Policies, and Measures

Debra Smith

CMG, Constraints Management Group LLC
Enumclaw, Washington

The St. Lucie Press/APICS Series on Constraints Management

S^t_L

St. Lucie Press

Boca Raton   London   New York   Washington, D.C.

Library of Congress Cataloging-in-Publication Data

Smith, Debra, 1952 —
    The Measurement Nightmare : how the theory of constraints can
    resolve conflicting strategies, policies, and measures / by Debra Smith.
    p. cm. - (APICS constraints management series)
    Includes index.
    ISBN 1-57444-246-5 (alk. paper)
    1. Theory of Constraints (Management). 2. Managerial accounting I. Title.
    II. St. Lucie Press/APICS series on constraints management.
HD69.T46 S65 2000
658.15′11—dc21
                                           99-053106
                                         CIP

Visit the CRC Press Web site at www.crcpress.com

© 2000 by CRC Press LLC

No claim to original U.S. Government works
International Standard Book Number 1-57444-246-5
Library of Congress Card Number 99-053106
Printed in the United States of America   4 5 6 7 8 9 0
Printed on acid-free paper

The Author

Debra Smith is a partner with Constraints Management Group, LLC, an international partnership committed to assisting organizations achieve breakthrough results and sustainable, ongoing improvements using the thought-process tools and application solutions offered through the Theory of Constraints.

Debra has extensive experience in public accounting, financial management in manufacturing companies, teaching at the university level, and consulting in the Theory of Constraints. She began working with the Avraham Y. Goldratt Institute in 1990 when she was an Associate Professor of Accounting at the University of Puget Sound in Tacoma, WA, and has been a licensed Academic Associate of the Institute since that time. She is responsible for original research in the field of Theory of Constraints applications in manufacturing environments and has created numerous courses and workshops integrating the Theory of Constraints and traditional manufacturing measurement and scheduling processes.

Her research has focused on understanding changes necessary in measurement and accounting and information systems to support continuous improvement processes in manufacturing. She is co-author of *The Theory of Constraints and Its Implications for Management Accounting*, an independent research study of the Theory of Constraints funded by the Institute of Management Accounting. This book is currently being used as a textbook in MBA course work in both the U.S. and Europe. Prior to consulting, Debra spent six years with the University of Puget Sound as an Associate Professor and one year as a visiting professor at The University of Washington. Prior to teaching, Ms. Smith worked in public accounting as a CPA for Touche, Ross & Company (now Deloitte, Touche) and spent nine years in publicly traded manufacturing firms, both as a division Controller and a Vice President of Finance and Operations. She is recognized, both nationally and internationally, as an authority on management accounting and is a noted speaker on the Theory of Constraints. Videos of her presentations are available through the web site for the Constraints Management Group, located at www.cmg-toc.com.

Introduction

Companies seeking to maximize return on investment are increasingly forced to compete in a global environment that requires dramatic gains in the following factors:

1. Increasing sales and market share
2. Reducing cycle or lead time
3. Increasing quality
4. Reducing inventory
5. Reducing costs

Companies that excel in these areas have the ability to compete based on these features rather than on price alone. This advantage gives them the ability to differentiate themselves in the marketplace. Company management teams have identified the above key factors as necessary to increase return on investment and have developed key initiatives centered on some or all five. Many of the above key factors have either formal programs or at the very least have been identified as work outcomes or targets for functional areas of the companies.

Programs such as Just-in-Time, Lean Manufacturing, and the Theory of Constraints' Drum-Buffer-Rope are all aimed at inventory and lead-time reductions. Total Quality Management, Statistical Process Control, ISO 9000 certification, and Six Sigma are all various forms of quality improvement programs that have been or are currently popular. Across-the-board cost reduction initiatives are standard fare in American business. Companies assign team leaders or champions to drive the programs throughout the organization. They spend tremendous amounts of time and money on external consulting services and in-house training programs. At the end of the day, the health of the business is measured based on return on investment, and accounting is called in to measure the results and evaluate the individual functional areas of the business' performance — which program delivered its result (inventory down, costs down, cycle time down, quality up, sales up) and which did not; which functional areas of the business did well and which did not; who and what improved and who and what failed to improve. The results are published, the feedback loop completed, and the next year's round of improvement programs and targets begins again, and we have missed the big picture. Why, with all of these wonderful programs, incredibly talented people, and huge investments of time and money, do we fail to make lasting and real bottom-line improvements?

The ability to implement an organization's strategy is dependent on aligning internal resources so that they act in concert to improve and execute the strategy. Resource contention between competing initiatives, programs, and investment decisions must be resolved and their interdependencies understood and prioritized. Improvements in one area cannot be gained at the expense of another area of the business, if both are necessary for the business to succeed. Unfortunately, that is precisely what happens when individual improvement programs are put in place at local levels. To achieve our inventory reduction goals, we cause stockouts and delays in manufacturing. To cut our costs, we harm our quality or ability to deliver on time. To ensure that one product or project is brought in on time, we expedite over other products or projects, causing them to be late or delayed. Accounting systems and financial and incentive measurements focused on local improvement or cost collection or allocation continue to be one of the biggest stumbling blocks to companies wishing to improve their financial performance with the above-mentioned improvement processes. This is because they fail to recognize the interdependencies of the local actions and programs on the performance of the business as whole.

Agreement on the need for a measurement system that encourages local actions in line with a company's bottom-line results is common, but it continues to be elusive. Traditional cost-accounting product cost allocation, using direct labor to assign overhead to the products with a focus on local labor and machine efficiencies, is at best irrelevant and at worst dysfunctional. Chapters 1, 2, 3, and 4 have all been written to show clearly and help managers explain to their own peers, bosses, and subordinates how organizational dysfunction is linked to common work practices, measures, and standard cost concepts. An organization in conflict with itself by definition is not aligned and cannot execute even the best strategy to its highest potential.

Management accounting theory has two basic underlying concepts. The first is the process of measuring, analyzing, interpreting, and communicating *information* that helps managers fulfill organizational objectives. The other is the effect on human behavior of what is measured and how it is interpreted. It truly reflects the age-old question of which came first, the chicken or the egg. Did the measure cause the behavior or did the behavior cause the measured results? I have come to the conclusion they are inseparable, and the decision as to what is measured, analyzed, interpreted, and communicated determines the behavior and ultimately the economic viability of the company. This is a cycle that in turn will dictate further decisions on what should be measured, analyzed, interpreted, and communicated. The circle can be a vicious death spiral or represent a path of continuous improvement

Note that "information" in the previous paragraph is italicized. It does not say cost accounting. Cost accounting is a technical, industry hybrid and process designed to satisfy generally accepted accounting principles (GAAP). Nowhere is it written (in the tax code or The Bible) that the same information used for GAAP must be used to make management decisions. Eli Goldratt, author of *The Goal*, has told companies for years to just quit using traditional cost accounting, but the unanswered questions of "What will we use instead?" and "How will we bridge to the change?" have not been answered to the satisfaction of most managers. Even beginning management accounting texts emphasize not using GAAP-compiled numbers to make management decisions. All management accounting texts make the following statement: *A company will profit maximize when it makes and sells the product with the highest contribution margin per unit of its scarce resource.* Goldratt did not discover anything new, but he did take the theory and develop the methodology to make it usable. The practical application is groundbreaking, and making the process sustainable is a continuing evolution.

The other premise of management accounting revolves around selecting relevant information for decision-making. In the final stages of the decision-making process, managers compare two or more alternative courses of action. The decision is based on the difference in the effect of each alternative on future performance. The following is management accounting's definition of relevant information, taken from *Introduction to Management Accounting*, ninth ed. (Horngren et al., Prentice Hall, 1993): "Relevant information is the predicted future costs and revenues that will differ among alternative actions. The existence of a limiting factor changes the basic assumptions underlying the cost and revenue opportunity of a potential action."

The methodology to examine the underlying assumptions of costs and revenues of two potential courses of actions is what this book is about. Using the fundamental concept of the Theory of Constraints to define relevant information is the basis of my work with companies and this book. The Theory of Constraints builds a practical platform for aligning key strategies with local actions and for maximizing the return on a given set of resources in both the short and long run. If you put these two "truths" together, you see clearly why the existence of a constraint changes what is considered relevant information. It is relevant because the constraint determines the future benefit that the entire company will experience.

In the early 1980s, experts in academia, industry, and consulting lined up to take shots at traditional cost accounting, but the lines became dramatically drawn as to what the "right" alternative was. Tremendous amounts of energy, money, and corporate resources have been expended to chase better costing information. Concepts such as activity-based costing, then activity-based management, and now economic value management have evolved to answer the deficiencies of absorption unit costing for decision-making. None of them has integrated or proved compatible with the improvement mechanisms and manufacturing philosophies of Total Quality Management, SPC, Just-in-Time, Kaizan, or the Theory of Constraints at a global level. As commonly implemented, they all create local optimization that puts cost centers in competition for resources and results in conflicting actions between departments. They all ignore the impact of the scarce resource, the constraint.

People want to do a good job. They will seek to measure their own performance. There are key measures, strategies, or policies that people will interpret and act to maximize, with or without a formal cost system. If management does not identify the measurement, strategy, or policy for people, they will make up their own, based on their perception of the objectives of the system. Companies who believe they have avoided the pitfalls of performance measurement systems because they do not have a formal system are in the worst case situation. Everyone in the organization is defining what a good job is from their local viewpoint of what good performance is locally.

The Theory of Constraints can provide a framework for the how-to steps for management accounting theory for profit maximization. The Theory of Constraints is based on the following five-step process:

1. Identify the constraint.
2. Decide how to exploit the constraint.
3. Subordinate everything else in the organization to the decision to exploit the constraint.
4. Elevate the constraint.
5. Start over by finding the new constraint.

Practically implementing the above how-to steps is based on the following baseline assumptions:

1. There are a few key leverage points in any interdependent system that determine the overall performance of any organization and can be identified.
2. Maximizing the contribution margin (sales dollars, truly variable costs) per unit of the constraining resource will maximize the system's profit. Truly variable is defined as any cost that has a direct one-for-one change with volume. Besides the obvious raw materials cost, other truly variable costs can include sales commissions, packaging material, and shipping costs, but *not* direct labor, with the exception of labor payment based on piece-rate production.

3. The reality is that constraints or bottlenecks exist. Either manage them or they will manage the organization and result in constant firefighting.
4. A logical connection can be made between managing the constraints and the effects the organization is experiencing (the fire fights are the symptoms). Effect-cause-effect logic can be used to diagram the current environment and pinpoint a core problem, the underlying cause or place that connects the symptoms. This is the place where implementing a solution would result in the elimination of many or all of the symptoms the organization is experiencing.
5. Focusing resource improvement (or simply measuring the efficiency of a non-constrained resource area) may result in some local area improvement but will not ensure that the overall performance of the organization will improve. In many instances, a local performance improvement can actually cause the total organizational performance to decay.
6. All organizations (other than Microsoft, perhaps) have limited resources. Even if there were no negative outcomes for optimizing local area performance, resources expended at non-constraint processes will not result in maximizing return on investment. Resources used to increase performance of the constraining resource will result in increased performance for the entire system, thereby maximizing the return on investment.
7. Most constraints are not physical limitations but are limitations created because of the beliefs or policies about how to staff, supply, maintain, and support the organization. Our assumptions on how an area or group of people must be managed can create many obstacles or limitations. Discovering flawed assumptions supporting a belief or policy can uncover limits or restrictions artificially imposed on the constraint area. Exposing flawed assumptions can allow an organization to challenge its method of resource management and improvement priorities and change its behavior. The change in behavior can increase the ability to exploit the constraining resource and increase total throughput without resource investment. Policy or "philosophy" constraints are part of an organization culture and are often unwritten. As such, they are even more difficult for organizations to challenge and change.
8. Tackling policy and culture constraints is similar to slaughtering sacred cows. Previously, a new prophet or zealot often ended up dying on the spears of the faithful. In order to tackle a universal belief (such as least unit cost measures), the logic of the negative effects of the behavior supporting the sacred cow must be clearly shown and discovered by the people who must make and adopt the new. The Theory of Constraint's thinking processes, the logical effect-cause-effect communication

process, were developed to identify and break non-physical constraints and to lead organizations through a systematic and repeatable process of change. It is the process for identifying what is relevant information for decision-making by creating a methodology that challenges the predicted results.

Many companies have experienced almost unbelievable gains from the Theory of Constraints. *The Theory of Constraints and Its Implications for Management Accounting* (Noreen, Smith, and Mackey) is full of the results of companies that successfully implemented and continued to innovate based on the five steps of TOC. Based on my research and recent experience with clients, success is limited because of the failure to complete step three — subordinate everything else in the organization to the decision to exploit the constraint. If the organization identifies the key area for managing throughput, then they must communicate to all supporting areas how their actions and measures must change to support exploitation of the constrained capacity resource. In addition, there must be a system to create real-time feedback on when, where, and what is not subordinating, including policy constraints. These are the causes of delays or downtime at the constraint. Disagreement about how or where to subordinate causes delay. Delay causes disruption, and disruption causes lost opportunity for throughput. All non-constraint areas of the company must understand how they impact the constraint in order to take actions that enhance or maintain the constraint's performance.

Chapter 5 explains a basic reference environment for implementing TOC in a manufacturing environment. Using Chapter 5 as a reference environment, the design and implementation of a feedback loop to practically measure and communicate the causes of delays or downtime are discussed in detail in Chapters 6 and 7. The ability to focus the supporting resources so they can align their actions in day-to-day operations and continuously improve their ability to subordinate allows a company to exploit its constrained resource. You cannot have consistent exploitation without consistent subordination in an interdependent system.

The accounting profession has made recent attempts to address the shortfalls of traditional absorption-based cost accounting by introducing "new" costing methods such as activity-based costing and economic value added. I propose that these new methods have failed to recognize the basic difference between product costing for financial statement purposes and collecting management information to make real-time decisions at the local operations level and strategic decisions for future action. In the case of real-time decisions on the floor, the conflict continues to be measuring local optimization vs. global optimization. It is as simple as, "Tell me how you measure me, and I'll tell you how I will behave." People will take actions to maximize their measures. If their measure is in conflict with what is necessary to optimize global performance, the employee is faced with an immediate conflict, the result of which is fighting fires throughout the organization. If I take an action that is good for my area and your area has to clean up the result or react to the effect by passing the fire fight on to another area, delay and dysfunction increase in the system. Often the solution to a local fire fight simply lights another fire. The solution is to align day-to-day management decisions of all resources with the strategic objective of exploiting the organization's constraint. This is my definition of relevant management accounting information for decision-making, and I believe that the Theory of Constraints can be used as the practical framework.

In the case of using absorption-based costing tools to evaluate strategic decisions, the conflict is the attempt to measure a global strategic fixed-cost investment with a short-term cost tool designed to assign product cost or value. The fixed investment cost exists because of a strategic decision to invest in the resource for the long term. It has no relation to volume or activity-driven actions at a local level in the short run. This conflict can result in the under-utilization of a strategic resource because of the wish of a local area to avoid the cost allocation associated with the resource. The negative effect to the company is magnified if the area manager can purchase the resource outside at a lower "cost". This is one of the basic issues of flawed transfer pricing and the popular notion of local "profit" centers. Again, it is an example of a local action not being aligned with the strategic investment to maximize the global goal because of the measurement of cost assignment to the local area.

Absorption accounting has a significant purpose of satisfying outside reporting requirements, and most academics and many practitioners agree that it is not the appropriate vehicle for internal management decisions. Financial cost accounting is a screwdriver, and we should use it to put in screws. Yet, we continue to try to modify the tool so it also pounds in nails. It is time to put some very basic premises out and allow company management and the management accounting profession to use their common sense and re-examine what every introductory management accounting textbook since the 1960s has made perfectly clear. Management accounting should provide information to make local and strategic decisions and measure key results that are aligned with the global goal of the company.

The behavioral implications of management accounting are critical and, in all significant respects, more important than rearranging the costs. All measures, work practices, and reporting need to reinforce the behavior a company is seeking from its workforce. This is especially true when a company is attempting to change behavior across the organization through approaches such as the Theory of Constraints, Kaizan, Lean Manufacturing, or Total Quality Management.

Instead of trying to turn absorption cost accounting into relevant data, this book proposes a much simpler solution. Revolve the company reporting around relevant measures and strategic information and convert direct-costing information at the month end to absorption costing using a simple bridge. This approach is known by every CPA practice in the U.S. that deals with small manufacturing firms that supposedly have not been sophisticated enough to have invested millions of dollars to track overhead by product on a daily, hourly, or minute basis. The variance reporting that is generated at the end of every month, purported to control costs, is not useful or timely and actually puts departments into conflict with each other and the overall goal of maximizing throughput at a minimum cash outflow.

This book proposes a radically different approach from the current philosophy of the major consulting and public accounting industries, and, as such, it will not be popular with some of them. Basically, this approach is simple, effective, elegant, and inexpensive and requires no software investment. Chapter 8 is a basic how-to for converting direct cost or "throughput accounting" statements to GAAP financial statements using standard cost accounting.

If the concept is well established, then why has the concept has been totally overlooked except by a few lone voices in the field of management accounting? There are six basic reasons:

1. Accounting systems have been built to capture data necessary for cost accounting and financial statement preparation. This system is firmly entrenched and used to train all accounting personnel when they are hired. Their jobs revolve around this costing system. Operations auditing revolves around compliance with the existing system.

2. Accounting education and accreditation have focused on certified public accounting, and, as a result, accounting degrees require only one quarter or one semester of management accounting, much of which is dedicated to standard absorption cost accounting, which is a financial accounting concept, not a management accounting concept.

3. All business and engineering education teaches students to make management decisions using financial statement information. At least accountants know the information can lead to erroneous decisions.

4. Accounting is a technical field. Operations managers cannot verbalize the negative ramifications of their actions and decisions using the cost information, and the accountants that provide it do not understand the consequences to global operations of focusing on local optimization measures.

5. Because of the above, accountants lack the training or methodology to tackle redesigning their accounting system to emphasize management information rather than financial statement generation. They do not know how or where to begin. There is a basic belief, no matter how erroneous, that the information generated is necessary to control costs.

6. There has been no practical alternative to local optima measures based on resource efficiency. People have not had the ability to logically link their actions to company return on investment. This book will explain how the Theory of Constraints can be used to address this barrier. This can no longer be used as a valid excuse to manage with invalid information.

When I spoke recently at Utah State University's Partners in Business Symposium, I presented my research and proposed changes in accounting education and practice and was delightfully surprised by the reaction from faculty and practitioners alike, who came to the conclusion that current practices are "heresy", even though they were reluctant to admit it. The time has come to expose the flawed assumptions underlying our current internal reporting. Competition demands it. The first need is the recognition that no matter what costing method a company uses, at the end of the year you will have the same cash, assets, liabilities, workforce, and market. But, the method you use will lead you to very different (often opposite) strategic decisions. *If the decisions are opposite, then only one of them can be optimal, and it is dependent on the company-specific environment, the environment reflected by the company's constraint.*

The first purpose of this book is to show clearly the current dilemma companies face with their current measurement, accounting, and management information systems. In it, I discuss the basic premises and evolution of the Theory of Constraints and how it can be used to create a practical bridge between relevant information for decision-making at local levels and global return on investment. The second purpose of this book is to examine what measures are needed on a manufacturing floor to perfectly align real-time action at local levels with the global goal of maximizing throughput. The book describes practical examples of measurement systems, devised around Drum-Buffer-Rope scheduling, and the methodology used by the companies to devise their new measurements and delete measurements and reporting not aligned with the global goal and behavior the company wishes to reinforce. The third purpose is to expose the simple method for converting a direct-costing system to absorption costing to satisfy GAAP and external reporting requirements. The basic issues preventing us from taking a simple approach to the problem include:

1. Costs sunk in our existing accounting system
2. Re-education of our current accounting and management staff
3. Believing that accounting financial statements are to be used for decision-making
4. Believing that a simple solution cannot exist (we are a complex company)
5. Inertia

The fourth purpose of this book is the subject of Chapter 9 — to explore four basic financial strategic decisions from a Theory of Constraints and direct-costing approach:

1. Product emphasis
2. Capital investment and process improvement
3. Adding a product or a market niche
4. Deleting a product

The process for making a decision regarding the deletion or addition of a product can be extrapolated to include a division or subsidiary. Specific examples, from actual company cases, are used to illustrate the strategic consequences of various costing approaches. The cases are designed to help the reader discover why absorption costing is fundamentally flawed and how an approach using direct and incremental costing with an emphasis on the Theory of Constraints has been and continues to be the only sound approach to these management accounting decisions. One of the cases in Chapter 9 illustrates how one company was able to align their short-term profit maximization to best fulfill their long-term market strategy. By understanding and managing the current constraining resource, they could maximize the short-run profits. This allowed them the time necessary to identify where to invest to realign their assets and move the internal resource constraint to enable them to best support and exploit their long-term market strategy. The case clearly demonstrates the predictable negative profit impact resulting from product emphasis and pricing decisions, capital investment decisions, and the decision to delete a product based on analysis using a combination of traditional full-absorption costing, activity-based costing, and traditional direct-costing information. The company failed to consider the organization's limiting resource, and the result was a complete misalignment of actions taken to design a market strategy to accomplish the goal of a favorable return on investment.

The fifth purpose for the book is to address the issue of executive incentive plans and the inherent conflict in attempts to align long-term and short-term profit objectives. Chapter 10 examines how to use the TOC concepts and tools to integrate economic value management principles to design executive incentive systems based on return on investment, both long and short term. Using direct costing for inventory valuation corrects the distortions of standard cost accounting and negates the opportunity to create false "profit" through inventory manipulation but does not address the long-term vision. As companies move further into an environment of low inventories of work in process and finished goods, the distortion of traditional standard cost accounting becomes less and less an issue. The remaining hurdle is to restate financial statement profit to best align executive strategy and decision-making with both short- and long-term results.

How do you allocate resources? How do you measure performance by top management on the use of these resources? How do you pay or reward the management group for performance? Consulting firms are attempting to answer these questions using economic value management to adjust standard financial accounting statements. These adjustments have four major objectives and are compatible with TOC:

1. Move from an accrual basis to a cash basis to arrive at the correct timing of an expenditure — for example, accrual of bad debt reserve vs. write-off of bad debts.
2. Remove the impact of one-time events — work stoppages, gain on sale of securities.
3. Remove the effect of debt financing and become a fully equity-financed firm — tax advantage of interest expense, tax impact of interest income.
4. Move from an accounting life of an asset to an economic life — increase or decrease the asset life of machinery.

If I could sum up the Theory of Constraints from my 12 years of research, experimentation, success, and failure, it would simply be two words: *focus* and *leverage*. The Theory of Constraints guides management toward where and how they should focus resources to leverage return on investment and how the approach should be continuously monitored and communicated to the rest of the organization to act on to create continuous improvement. If you figure out how to accomplish the above, then you have figured out the Theory of Constraints and you have created a continuous learning organization. It is the quest and the reward and explains why the people in the organization are the key. Unfortunately people are also the most undervalued asset in corporate America. They do not even appear on the balance sheet, yet without them a company has no ability to return value on its balance sheet investment. This is the next step in creating and measuring value — the ability to measure, assign worth to, and reward managers for building human capital.

Contents

About APICS

APICS, The Educational Society for Resource Management, is an international, not-for-profit organization offering a full range of programs and materials focusing on individual and organizational education, standards of excellence, and integrated resource management topics. These resources, developed under the direction of integrated resource management experts, are available at local, regional, and national levels. Since 1957, hundreds of thousands of professionals have relied on APICS as a source for educational products and services.

- **APICS Certification Programs**—APICS offers two internationally recognized certification programs, Certified in Production and Inventory Management (CPIM) and Certified in Integrated Resource Management (CIRM), known around the world as standards of professional competence in business and manufacturing.
- *APICS Educational Materials Catalog*—This catalog contains books, courseware, proceedings, reprints, training materials, and videos developed by industry experts and available to members at a discount.
- *APICS—The Performance Advantage*—This monthly, four-color magazine addresses the educational and resource management needs of manufacturing professionals.
- *APICS Business Outlook Index*—Designed to take economic analysis a step beyond current surveys, the index is a monthly manufacturing-based survey report based on confidential production, sales, and inventory data from APICS-related companies.
- Chapters—APICS' more than 270 chapters provide leadership, learning, and networking opportunities at the local level.

- **Educational Opportunities**—Held around the country, APICS' International Conference and Exhibition, workshops, and symposia offer you numerous opportunities to learn from your peers and management experts.
- **Employment Referral Program**—A cost-effective way to reach a targeted network of resource management professionals, this program pairs qualified job candidates with interested companies.
- **SIGs**—These member groups develop specialized educational programs and resources for seven specific industry and interest areas.
- **Web Site**—The APICS Web site at http://www.apics.org enables you to explore the wide range of information available on APICS' membership, certification, and educational offerings.
- **Member Services**—Members enjoy a dedicated inquiry service, insurance, a retirement plan, and more.

For more information on APICS programs, services, or membership, call APICS Customer Service at (800) 444-2742 or (703) 237-8344 or visit http://www.apics.org on the World Wide Web.

1

Unbelievable Decisions by Companies You Would Know if I Could Name Them

This chapter will read like *Dilbert* but is no joke. The following situations involve companies with which I have been personally involved, and I have first-hand knowledge regarding the decisions and outcomes. I used to tell these stories to my students, clients, and people who attended my seminars. My students thought I made them up because, in their words, "No one could be that stupid." People who work in industry simply nod their heads in sad agreement and tell me equally strange and disturbing tales from their own companies or companies they have previously worked for. No matter how ridiculous people's actions appear, I can consistently tie their actions to their honest attempts to comply with measurements, policies, and strategies, either written or unwritten. Standard cost accounting measures require logical people to act in ways that do not make logical sense.

Now sit back and enjoy the following true stories. These examples vividly confirm the widespread need for coherent change, driven by a simple, repeatable holistic approach to managing the organization. My work is centered on how to cause subordination to the decision to exploit the scarce resource, the constraint. In order to accomplish subordination, measures, policies, strategies, and beliefs must be aligned so people can make decisions and take action without putting themselves in conflict with the "system" vs. the interdependence issues around the constraint. There must be a clear understanding of how their local action will affect the constraining resource. What is good for exploiting the constraining resource is good for the company. The inverse is just as true. What harms the ability to exploit the constraining resource harms the company. The stories presented here clearly demonstrate these principles.

Several years ago I was involved with a venture capital group that purchased a regional, building-products manufacturing company. Their intent was to take the brand national. The company had a solid reputation for quality and on-time delivery, had name-brand recognition on the East Coast, and had the number one market share in the south. Within two years, they achieved an annual growth trend of 25% in a national market growing at less than 2%. Management decided to explore the Theory of Constraints (TOC) as a method to increase production to keep up with their increasing market demand without major fixed-asset expenditures. Upon visiting the plant, I was given a tour by the president of the company, who explained the manufacturing facilities as a process plant. Mixers batched the product, and the filling line squeezed the product into tubes, which were packed in cases and moved on to shipping. The president proudly explained their recent acquisition of an automatic case packer.

The board of directors had approved the acquisition because it reduced direct labor costs and increased the labor efficiency of the entire plant. The case packer replaced two laborers and allowed the filling line to run at its highest setting. The automatic case packer was faster by about 20% than hand packing, and throughput (selling price – raw materials × volume per hour) on the filling line was expected to increase from $3750 per machine hour to $4500 per machine hour. The approximate $40,000 annual reduction in labor and $1,560,000 increased throughput ($750/hour increase × 2080 hours annually) were used to justify the $250,000 purchase price of the automatic case packer.

When I arrived, the case packer was down and so was the filling line. Whenever the case packer did not operate, the filling line had to be shut down because there was no place for the product to go. It was obvious that the maintenance people and the filling-line operator understood the importance of getting the case packer up and running. The president explained that everyone in the plant understood that the filling line was the bottleneck. When operating, the filling line contributed $4500 throughput per machine hour. He pointed out that he understood throughput to be sales minus raw materials, and that they could currently ship anything they could produce. In fact, I was there to help them expand their production so backorders did not become a serious problem. I asked the maintenance man how often the case packer broke down, on average. He told me it was usually down at least 10 hours a week. I asked what it was like at the plant before they got the case packer. He explained that he had spent a lot less time at the plant; in fact, the time spent keeping the case packer running increased overtime dramatically. His base rate of pay was twice the cost of the labor replaced by the automatic case packer. The hourly overtime expense for maintenance was three times as expensive as the hourly direct labor expense that was saved.

The loss of throughput due to downtime on the case packer was at least 10% more than the gain in throughput from running the filling line faster. An approximate weekly loss of at least $15,000 of throughput — (40 hours × $3750) – (30 hours × $4500) — was due to the automation of case packing. The increased cost of overtime for maintenance was 20% of the $40,000 labor savings used to justify the equipment purchase and routinely stretched maintenance's ability to keep up with routine work in the shop. Maintenance cost did not have an impact on direct labor efficiencies because maintenance is considered an indirect overhead cost. On the surface, the measures told the president the company was in better shape; however, the growing production backlog and bottom line told him otherwise.

It took a pencil and paper to convince the president that the automatic case packer had actually reduced throughput. The solution was simple. In order to exploit the constraining resource, product must be packed as it comes off the filling line. In order to pack product when the automatic case packer was down, the plant would need to install a diverter to move the product to a table where two people could be hired to pack product. If, on average, the case packer was inoperable 10 hours a week and hand packing could keep the filling line operating at a rate of $3750 of throughput per hour, then the company could receive $37,500 more every week by hiring two people for $800 a week. The number one stumbling block was the idea of increasing headcount and the resulting decline in the labor efficiencies. There was also the problem of what to do with the people when the automatic case packer was operating. My answer: gardening, cleaning, painting, free car washing for employees! Anything would be worth their availability to deliver the $1,910,000 ($3750 hourly throughput × 10 hours × 52 weeks – $40,0000 additional labor cost) of throughput annually. That was the annual bottom-line impact. I did agree, though, that their reported labor efficiencies would go down.

One of the basic lessons I learned from the automatic case packer was the predictable effect of coupling a process to the constrained resource. If a process is coupled, either before or after, and it cannot be decoupled from the constraining resource, any downtime on the process coupled is downtime at the constraint. If the process cannot be decoupled, downtime at the constrained resource will go up. Coupling at the front of the process destroys the ability to buffer the constrained resource. The majority of automation projects are justified by a reduction of labor costs or raw material costs or the elimination of process time before or after the constraint, without regard to the impact on throughput of the constraint. The reduction of process time at any process other than the constraining resource does not increase the rate of throughput of the plant. In the above instance, even though the intent was to increase the constraining resources rate of throughput, the opposite happened because the delays or disruptions at the case packer were passed on to the constraint.

Any justification of a process improvement must address the impact on the throughput rate of the constraint. This can be equated to requiring an "environmental impact statement", with the environment of the constraint and all strategic buffers designed to protect the constraint as the subjects of the analysis. The strategic buffers and constrained resource impact statement should become standard operating procedure for a capital expense improvement or a process change anywhere in the system. This concept is more fully explored in Chapter 7.

A year later, the building-products manufacturing company had become so successful that they were purchased by one of the giants in their industry (identified here as Giant). Why? Because their product was carried in Giant's retail stores as a premium brand, it was delivered to Giant's distribution center on time, and customers requested it because of its reputation for high quality at a reasonable price. The negotiation started out as a request to contract pack Giant's brand of product and ended in the acquisition of the small company. Thus began the demise of a great little company, and all of the reasons why they had been acquired were immediately in jeopardy. Why? Giant's accounting information used for decision-making and measures did not jive with their TOC environment.

This story continues during the due diligence before the acquisition, when the acquirer snoops through the books of the company to be acquired to decide if the company really is what it claims to be. Both companies in our story purchased chemical raw materials from the same national source, and Giant purchased vast quantities of chemicals. Both companies were shocked to discover that the small company's cost for raw materials was 8% less than Giant's best price from the same supplier. The supplier explained that the price had been negotiated because the small company always paid within 10 days of receipt and the large company never paid in less than 60 days. This required the supplier to borrow money for 50 days longer to do business with Giant. Terms are part of price.

Giant had adopted a policy to maximize the return on cash and did not pay any vendor in less than 60 days. The average earnings on the cash invested by Giant was approximately 5% annually. The question that needs to be asked, then, is what is Giant's business? Is it to invest "excess" cash in financial markets or to manufacture and distribute retail building products? According to the 1995 financial statements (the year of the acquisition) and assuming the chemical component of raw materials at only 5% of total cost of operating expenses, 8% savings would increase their bottom line by over $12,500,000. Their entire interest expense for the year was less than $2,500,000. This is not the question Giant asked themselves, though; instead, Giant screamed at their purchasing agent and the supplier. This had no impact on the price nor did it cause a change in Giant's policy. The only result was an increase in the cost of raw materials to the acquired "new division" at the end of the 6-month purchase contract.

Another decision made by Giant, with major negative ramifications, was their decision to implement across-the-board cost cutting and a headcount reduction. How this decision came about reflects a good management decision regarding a major customer and a significant private-label contract. For numerous years, Giant had been a private-label supplier to a major national retail chain. The major national retail chain has the largest retail market share of this particular type of product, and the contract was a substantial portion of the revenue base of Giant's largest division. The major national retail chain put the entire business out for bid and informed Giant they could only regain the contract if they were able to meet the lowest bid price. The end result was that, in order to secure the contract, Giant had to accept a price decrease with an annual negative impact of $10 million dollars in sales revenue and ultimately net profit.

Giant made a good decision as far as meeting the lowest price and retaining the business. The manufacturing operations supporting the major national retail chain brand are highly automated, and the loss of the major national retail chain business would have left them with tremendous surplus capacity and result in a much larger loss than the $10 million reduction. The foolish decision was to mandate across-the-board cost cutting in which all divisions shared equally in absorbing the reduced income from the major national retail chain. This type of decision ignores a basic principle of physics and TOC — if you decrease the ability of the weakest link you decrease the ability of the entire organization. The small, recently acquired division was on track with 25% annual growth and was shipping every unit they could produce. Their growth was based on their demonstrated ability to meet customer demand with a quality product and short turn-around from order to delivery. Many of their national accounts were new, and a continuing business relationship was dependent on delivery of promises made regarding on-time delivery. In addition, the new division had no excess layers of management to cut, and they could not induce their suppliers to reduce raw-material prices; in fact they had just sustained the 8% increase in raw materials mentioned above. This left only three options:

1. Reduce the sales force.
2. Reduce direct labor.
3. Reformulate the product, sacrificing some quality features for lower cost ingredients.

Any of these options would seriously compromise the division's ability to meet its aggressive sales-growth targets and would harm throughput and net profit in both the short and long run.

This is just one example of the result of companies losing sight of the fact that a company is a chain of dependent events. Such examples also illustrate one of my main concerns about the implementation of stovepipe solutions from basically sound ideas such as Total Quality Management or reengineering without a Theory of Constraints focus. The five-step focusing process of TOC ensures that the cost-savings project does not harm the constraining resource by violating the ability to exploit the resource or by not subordinating other resources or departments to the decision to exploit the constraining resource. Installation of the automatic case packer and the exploitation of cash, which was obviously not the constraining resource, are examples of the ramifications of violating the exploitation and subordination decisions inherent in the TOC management philosophy. The across-the-board cuts in our example blatantly ignored the obvious and compromised the ability of the company to make money in the future.

When the finance department maximized their use of cash, the company missed maximizing the overall return on investment to the business. By maximizing the case-packing and labor efficiencies the company eliminated the bottleneck, reduced total throughput, and spent $250,000 to do it. By imposing an across-the-board cut, the constraining resource is cut equally with every other area. Negatively impacting the constraining resource negatively impacts the division's ability to generate throughput. The cost cut successfully derailed the new division's sales and profit plan for the year and seriously jeopardized all of the features that were attractive to Giant in the first place.

One of the most successful implementations of Drum-Buffer-Rope (DBR), the TOC methodology of plant scheduling, was initiated by a major producer of children's drawing supplies. This company is a division of a large holding company. Their success with DBR can be measured by the reduction of cycle time from 3 weeks to 5 days, work-in-process inventory reduction of 85%, and a finished goods inventory reduction of 70%. In addition, the company's on-time delivery rate improved from 75% to 99%. The implementation left a large finished goods warehouse empty and scrapped the plans for an additional warehouse to increase their ability to deliver on time. The implementation was regarded as an operations project and did not include any other part of the organization or corporate accounting. The director of customer service and the director of manufacturing asked me to meet with corporate accounting and explain how the product costing was causing a major problem between the company brand managers and the plant managers. The brand manager's incentives were based on brand gross profit, and the plant manager's incentives on maximizing inventory turns.

The current incentive system for the brand managers was based on the gross profit of the brand. The gross profit was computed as selling price less standard unit cost of goods sold. The brand managers were empowered to manage their slice of the business as an independent business. If they could procure goods or service outside the organization at a lower cost, they could act to secure the lower cost. This made the brand managers directly responsible for obtaining the lowest cost. The cost accounting system assigned cost to each unit of product based on the batch size. The brand in conflict was poster paint. The paint line is highly automated, and the time needed to set up to run is the same regardless of the number of units processed in a single batch. A color changeover requires the paint lines be cleaned before the next color batch can be produced.

Accounting had determined an optimal batch size to determine standard cost was 1000 gallons. Running a batch of 500 gallons would result in doubling the unit cost, and a batch of 250 gallons would quadruple the unit cost. Running low-volume colors at the optimum batch resulted in months of inventory.

Children like painting with blue, red, yellow, and green more than brown, and poster paints come in teeny tiny jars. An optimal batch of unpopular colors created a major surplus of inventory. Even worse, dictating an artificial batch size not tied to market demand increased the cycle time and inventory of all products. The plant managers recognized that producing the optimal standard cost batch would severely harm their bonus potential and lead them in the opposite direction from the TOC management philosophy they were practicing. Tying up plant capacity by producing to-fill finished goods made the plant less flexible in responding to market demand and threatened all of the gains from implementing the TOC scheduling philosphy of DBR. The plant managers understood their plants were highly automated, and the paint lines had sufficient excess capacity to reflect market demand without regard for minimizing setups. *The constraint was in the marketplace, not their operations.*

The plant managers understood the negative ramifications of having the brand managers buy the low-volume colors from outside sources. The entire industry had excess capacity, and long-term, high-volume purchase contracts could be secured for less than the standard cost of in-house production using low-volume batches. By outsourcing certain "unprofitable" colors, the company would be subsidizing their own competition and decreasing their own total net income. Regardless of the gallons of paint the plant produced, as long as they were in the paint business, they could not significantly decrease the plant asset base or monthly expenses. The plant managers had stumbled onto the major flaw in activity-based costing as it is routinely applied in industry. If you get rid of your low-volume products because they are "not profitable" from a fully burdened unit cost perspective, you really do not get rid of any of the production expenses except the truly variable costs. In an automated plant, truly variable costs translate to raw materials. Every penny in excess of the raw material cost increases your throughput, cash flow, and net income! Every penny over truly variable cost paid to your competitor decreases your net income and subsidizes your competitor's ability to beat you in the marketplace.

The plant, equipment, and personnel do not go away, whether they are allocated over four large-volume products or over the same four large-volume and some additional small-volume products. In fact, the "previously profitable" products become successively less profitable every time an "unprofitable" product is deleted. The same plant, personnel, and equipment are now spread over fewer units of products, and every unit of product experiences a real increase in unit cost. It is a fundamental mathematical principle — the smaller the denominator, the larger the cost per unit. But, if all of your costs are fixed (as they are in a highly automated plant) and you have excess capacity, then setups are *free* until you set up so many times that you have moved the constraint back into the plant. The equipment is there, the operators are there, and the entire plant overhead is there, regardless of whether it is used to make numerous setups and small batches or one large continuous batch to store in your warehouse! This is the basic premise of economic breakeven analysis, the backbone of management accounting and direct costing.

The director of operations and the director of customer service of this company had decided to have the plants produce minimum batches and maintain short cycle times and minimum inventories. This required that they explain to corporate accounting the unfavorable standard cost variances from running the "suboptimal batches" every month. In addition, the small-batch colors reported extremely unfavorable unit product cost and gross margin deterioration. Corporate accounting did not understand their explanations, but they were enthusiastic about the tremendous operations improvements. They understood that the cash flow increase, inventory turns increase, and decreased overtime expenses were directly related to the DBR implementation. The capital investment to accomplish the gains was minimal, and the funds for a major fixed-capital project had been returned to corporate. But, they could not understand how minimizing unit cost would not additionally help the plants.

I was asked to try to help bridge the gap between the two areas so the plant could continue to make small batches of less popular colors and stop brand managers from their plans to purchase the colors with "high unit costs" from outside sources. It was a frustrating several hours for all of us. Explaining the movement of product through the plant and the interrelationship of inventories, batch sizes, and cycle times was easy. The accountants understood how increasing batch sizes to an artificial optimum would deteriorate all of the TOC gains, but they could not understand how to keep track of plant and brand performance without standard cost-variance analysis by individual brand. They also could not articulate their new understanding to the rest of corporate accounting and construct a bridge between this new way of managing manufacturing and rewarding and measuring their brand managers' performance, but they clearly understood the negative impact on company net profit if the brand managers were allowed to purchase "lower cost" product from competitors in order to maximize their brands' gross profits and their incentive plans. It was a stalemate. This was 1995, and we were all frustrated. I could not give them a specific way to reconcile their accounting system to TOC, nor could I alleviate their fears of losing control of costs. This is common to numerous companies and has become the basis for the structure of my work around a way to communicate and bridge management accounting measures and TOC.

Any long-term approach to a holistic management philosophy, such as the Theory of Constraints, must include measurements and incentives that incorporate the valid concerns and obstacles of implementing the policy, measurement, and accounting changes necessary to support the new philosophical environment. You cannot just tell people it will be all right, trust me! Any process requiring a sweeping change, such as getting rid of a company's standard costing system, has to show the logical connections of why the new system will solve your problems and why the old one did not. Company personnel must be able to create the solution themselves so the system can continue to evolve, and they can continue to innovate it as conditions and circumstances change.

Purchasing is commonly measured on their ability to generate favorable purchase price variances. Many of the companies that I have been exposed to are part of the aerospace and military supply chain. One of the most blatant misuses of purchase price variance involves fixed-length military contracts. The fixed length of the contract leaves no doubt as to the program life of the product. It is commonly accepted in high-technology markets that product life-cycles are shrinking. Because standard accounting practice is to recognize purchase price variances in the financial statements in the period (month) they occur, they make a large, visible, and immediate impact, either positive or negative, on net income. The excess inventory, from a favorable buy, appears in the financial statements as an "asset" until it is either used or, in some cases, written off as obsolete. In the meantime, it takes up space, cash flow, and maintenance time and sends a false cost and performance measure throughout the system.

In one specific instance, the aerospace division of a Fortune 500 company that was responsible for a highly visible military weapons project made a buy ten times larger than the entire program life. This was done in order to receive a price that was four times better than a price for the realistic quantity that matched the program life. This came to light when the new chief financial officer started matching inventory parts to programs in an effort to understand how to begin an inventory reduction program. This particular transaction was only the tip of the iceberg. In order to maximize the performance measures for estimating, sales, and purchasing, buys of this nature were common. The estimating function needed the least-cost part to come up with the lowest bid, sales needed a least-cost part to get the order, and purchasing needed the most favorable purchase price variance. The consequences of the action, the inventory write-off, would come at the end of the program, sometimes years down the road.

Unfortunately for the CFO and the company, his program was a day late and a dollar short. The aerospace downturn in 1994/95 left the company and the entire industry in the vulnerable position of having excess capacity or high fixed costs and competing for fewer contracts. Some programs were terminated, and many had their lives reduced, causing companies to reevaluate their inventory and bidding practices. From the perspective of a unit-cost world, new program costs and existing program costs increased dramatically at the company. The fixed-cost portion of the cost pool remained constant from a total-dollar perspective but increased dramatically on a per-unit basis when spread over the remaining programs' dwindling volume base. New programs reflected the higher overhead rates, and the division routinely lost out on bids to smaller job shops not trapped in the death spiral of allocating higher and higher overhead rates. Such a dilemma can be stated as: "In order to get the new business, I must meet the competitive bid price, but to maintain my margins I must bid at a price that covers my current overhead rate. Every time I lose another bid, the overhead rate increases again, because there is less volume to spread the fixed costs over and more programs look like losers that must be eliminated." In 1996, the division was divested to a competitor for the depleted value of the remaining programs, inventory, and equipment. Pricing product based on any form of absorption costing, including activity-based costing, has this predictable negative result when the incremental cost of the product is ignored. The cases in Chapter 9 clearly demonstrate the points of this story.

One of the most common measures in use today is units per man-hour. This measure is a summary of standard costing's use of standard labor hours and standard labor rates, resulting in labor variance analysis and decisions designed to improve this measure. It seems intuitive to American managers that if parts per man-hour go up, the company's position should be improving. If I have learned anything from the Theory of Constraints it is the value of checking your assumptions. *Flawed assumptions invariably lead to flawed behavior and flawed outcomes*, no matter how well accepted the premise is by the general populace. Didn't Columbus' generation widely believe he would eventually sail off the edge of the world? The negative impacts on throughput and ultimately net profit are legion and were demonstrated in the first story, but the following example is so clearly traceable to the measure of output per man-hour that the idea bears repeating.

In the summer of 1997, I began a TOC product-solution implementation with the first plant of multi-plant division of a publicly traded firm. The plant buys processed material from a sister plant and weaves the material into cloth. The cloth is then cleaned, coated, slit, sheared. The sheared pieces can then be assembled with other purchased parts into a finished product or sold as sheared pieces in kits. After showing the movie "The Goal" and providing a basic introduction to the idea of a constraint, I began the implementation by teaching the team two of the thought-process tools:

1. Clouds — how to diagram conflict logically and find a solution
2. Negative branches — how to link ideas or events clearly to negative outcomes

By the middle of the second day, my mildly interested team started to get excited, especially the plant manager. Two months prior, an edict had come from the division's new vice president to increase units per man-hour by cutting direct labor at the looms. Not only were the looms the most expensive equipment in the plant, but they were also widely recognized as being the constraint. The plant was not making money, their on-time delivery was 70%, and, to make matters worse, they were a first-tier supplier and their customer pulled daily from their inventory. If the order was not available, the plant did not get a second chance. The second-tier supplier was used instead, and the plant permanently lost that throughput opportunity. In addition, their poor on-time delivery performance would negatively impact their chances of retaining the contract when it expired in 12 months. The contract bid price was based on the company's belief that they could supply 100% of the volume, so all of labor and overhead variances were unfavorable. The key performance indicator, reflecting both of these unfavorable variances, was units per man-hour at the looms.

Based on reviewing plant and labor operations, the only potential place to cut labor costs was in the highly automated area of weaving. The slitting, shearing, and winding machines required one operator per machine. The high-speed looms, although labor intensive to set up, ran on average 20 to 30 days between setups. The loom operators were highly skilled and received the highest wage rate (the industry estimates it takes 6 to 8 years to create a journeyman weaver). The plant's 18 looms ran 24 hours a day, 7 days a week, and the ratio of looms to weaver was three to one. The decision was to reduce the loom operators from six per shift to four per shift. The looms were also the constraint.

I had just finished explaining to the team how throughput of the entire plant is dictated by the constraint. Any reduction of the constraint decreases the throughput of the entire plant; on-time delivery will go down, overtime will go up, and the rest of the plant will experience random starvation; every order will appear "hot" and the bottleneck will appear to float around the plant. They went wild. They instantly made the connection to the effects they had been seeing during the last two months after the decision had been made to decrease the number of loom operators. Overtime had increased in every department, and shipments had dropped because product was not available when the customer called for a pickup. Downtime at the looms had increased substantially, and the plant manager was under fire from corporate to explain the growing, negative profit-and-loss performance and the deteriorating on-time delivery performance during the last two months. Units per man-hour at the looms had increased. The output of yard of cloth as a proportion of direct labor was higher than it had been previously but total output of the looms was down.

By decreasing the labor by half, the looms experienced approximately a 25% increase in downtime, which meant that the number of units per man-hour went up by 25% but the entire throughput of the plant went down by 25%. We spent the next two hours creating an effect-cause-effect logic tree, known as a negative branch, for the vice president. The negative branch clearly and simply linked the effect-cause-effect logic of the reduction in weaving workforce to the increase in plantwide overtime and shipment loss and ultimately to the disastrous net-profit effect. The division controller was part of the implementation team, and the negative branch was corrected the next day to show the actual dollar impact of each of the negative effects and the cumulative profit/loss over the previous two months.

On the spot, the plant manager and the controller made the decision to re-staff the looms immediately. Luckily, the plant manager had retained all of the loom operators in different areas of the plant, replacing less skilled employees with the weavers. If the weavers had been terminated, the plant would not have been able to recover in any short-run time frame.

The following is roughly the logic of the negative branch presented to the vice president: If the looms are the constraining resource and the looms feed all subsequent operations, then the plant shipments are dependent on the capacity of the looms. If a loom breaks a wire or tangles or the creel runs out of wire, it must be re-threaded. If a loom must be re-threaded, it must be shut down, and, if breaks, tangles, and creel-outs happen randomly on all shifts, then multiple machines can need operator attention at any one time.

If it takes 24 hours to complete a loom changeover and looms run from 20 to 30 days, depending on the wire size, and if the company has 18 looms, then multiple looms may need setups at the same time. If multiple looms need to be set up and shipments are in danger of being late and operators are available to work overtime, then overtime at the looms goes up.

If multiple machines need operator attention at any one time and multiple looms need setups at the same time and the number of available loom operators is decreased by 50%, then loom downtime will increase. If loom downtime increases and all processes downstream use product produced at the looms, then processes downstream from the constraint will starve. If processes downstream from the constraint starve and the customer orders are in danger of not shipping and downstream processes have excess machine capacity that can be staffed with overtime, then the downstream processes will run overtime to try to catch up when the material arrives at their stations. If the downstream processes attempt to recover schedule disruptions with overtime to get the product out, then overtime increases at processes downstream from the constraint.

If overtime at the looms goes up and overtime at the processes downstream from the looms goes up, then the total labor expense goes up. If throughput at the constraint (the looms) goes down and the plant's ability to ship product is dependent on the constraint, then increasing downtime at the constraint causes missed shipments. If shipments are missed, net income goes down. If labor costs increase, net profit goes down. If shipments are missed and there is a second-tier supplier for the product, then the sales opportunity is lost forever.

If shipments are missed, then on-time delivery (OTD) performance deteriorates. If the plant OTD performance deteriorates and next year's contract is dependent upon OTD as well as price, then the plant is at risk of losing their contract as a first-tier supplier. If the contract as a first-tier supplier is 80% of the sales volume of the plant, then the plant risks ceasing to be viable within one year.

The logic backed up by the controller's numbers made common sense to the vice president. Within two weeks, things were back up to their previous performance levels, OTD was at 70%, and the plant was in a breakeven position. We went back to work on implementing the TOC production scheduling solution, DBR, with a very enthusiastic implementation team. They felt empowered. They had made the logical connections to their actions to exploit the faulty measure and the negative impact of not subordinating to exploiting the constraint. By failing to subordinate staffing decisions to allow exploitation of the looms (the constraint), they experienced two months of dramatically deteriorating net profit effects and faced the very real possibility of plant closure in less than a year. The plant manager and the supervisors believed the negative effects experienced throughout the plant were tied to the decision regarding staffing of the looms, but they were unable to break the idea down into small enough logical connections to communicate it clearly to corporate.

The vice president did not understand that maximizing the output per unit of labor hour of the constraint was counterproductive to making money. Maximizing least cost per unit of output is not the same as maximizing throughput dollars. The measure they chose did not reflect exploiting the looms. The company chose a measure to exploit direct labor input per output of the looms, not the overall output of the looms. The cost of a loom is $250,000, and the cost of a laborer was $15 per hour. The company invested in the looms so they could earn a return on the investment by making and selling product. The question is not "How can we minimize our labor investment in the loom area?" The question is "How much labor do we need to maximize our return on our investment in the plant?" If the looms are the constraint, maximizing the return on investment of the looms is the same as maximizing the return on investment in the plant. This scenario reminds me of the *Dilbert* cartoon in which Dilbert is trying to convince his boss to examine the idea of spending money to make money.

The biggest barrier to communication is the inability to explain our intuition in such a way that the undesirable effects being experienced are clearly linked to the root cause. This is especially true when the "causes" are being analyzed at a level or multiple levels removed from the cause of the chaos. Corporate accounting generates and mid-level management uses the "symptom-generated" variances, measures, and data of individual cost centers to draw their conclusions. Stated simply, here is the obvious: Using man-hours as a driver or gauge for the productivity of an automated constraint is illogical. The throughput of the constraint is tied to the time the constraint is up and producing product that is due now. Let me repeat "due now" — that is precisely why the next two stories are critical to understanding measures designed around the constraint. The first is a subordination measure for a plant support function designed to exploit the constraint. The second revolves around the cost beliefs commonly associated with setups.

During my teaching days, I designed an advanced management accounting class to include an interactive project with local companies. My students were taught TOC thought processes as part of the curriculum and then conducted a month-long field investigation. The objective was to identify a company's constraint and to communicate that constraint to the company, in addition to recommending how to exploit and subordinate other areas to the exploitation of the constraint to maximize throughput with the minimum inventory. The students delivered written and oral reports to the company management on their findings. One of the companies adopted my students' work and bought into the idea of exploiting the constraint and subordinating the measures of supporting resources to show their contribution to exploiting the constraint. They asked me to come in and evaluate their efforts. The plant was a small aerospace subsidiary of a multi-national conglomerate. I add this so you will understand we were dealing with a high-tech process and Ivy League-trained managers. This was a relatively sophisticated operation.

The constraint was a sophisticated and expensive piece of machinery designed to cut patterns in fiber mesh cloth for aerospace composite parts. The machine required constant maintenance and was repeatedly down for any number of mechanical failures. To be certain that maintenance subordinated itself to supporting the constraint, the maintenance team was measured on fast response time and how quickly they got the machinery up and running. The result was fast repair … and quick breakdown. We changed the measure to how long the machine stayed up between breakdowns. Both measures appeared to satisfy the intent to exploit the constraint, but the latter had the objective of overall up time at the constraint vs. the "jury-rig" focus the maintenance team had adopted. The maintenance team had not been given all of the information. In fact, they had not been consulted as to what the measurement should be, only what it was.

The objective was not simply to repair the machine quickly, but to repair the machine to maximize its run time. Maximizing run time quickly led maintenance to adopt a different set of actions. The maintenance team identified the new measure themselves when they addressed the questions, "Why was the machine continually down, and what could be done differently to impact total up time?" The area subordinating understands the best possible actions to take to ensure exploiting the constraint resource and potential, existing conflicts. Their participation in the design and ultimately the decision of when and how to act is the best way to approach new subordination measures. This requires that they are educated in the objectives of TOC and are given the ability to identify and communicate programs, demands, actions, or measures that exist in their area that would put them in conflict with the decision to exploit the constrained area.

When implementing TOC's finite production scheduling method (Drum-Buffer-Rope), a belief about batch sizes often surfaces and impacts identification of the constraint. During an implementation of DBR at the cloth manufacturer, the implementation team was split as to where the constraint resided. Remember, the first step in TOC is to identify the constraint so you can then decide how to exploit it. Weaving was convinced their looms were the constraint, and the rest of the plant was convinced it was in the slitting operation. The two operations following the slitting operation were routinely either flooded or starved. This led the supervisor of slitting and the operations downstream to believe slitting was the constraint. The first clue that the bottleneck was a policy constraint and not a physical constraint was *the alternate flooding and starving* of the downstream processes, not just continual starvation. A policy constraint is a practice or policy regarding how to manage a resource, not the actual physical capacity of the resource. Either slit rolls arrived very early or very late at both downstream workstations. Logically, if material is arriving early and late, the time spent running product early could have been spent producing product due now. If something arrives early, there must be excess capacity. The capacity used to run product early is wasted if it could be used to produce product that is late. This clearly shows a lack of synchronization.

There were two policies constraining slitting. The first was the decision to run large batch sizes at the slitters and to dedicate the entire batch to either final assembly or shearing despite the fact that both downstream processes used the same parts. The plant took on a "V" configuration at slitting. Slit cloth could either be sold as raw pieces or assembled with purchased parts and sold as finished-good product. If five different material types must be slit to feed the downstream processes and any single missing item stops assembly, then decreasing the batch size by half allows the slitters to feed the downstream process in half the cycle time. In other words, a batch size that requires a day of run time to produce one part would take five days to fill a complement of all parts needed for the assembly process to begin. Decreasing the batch size by half allows the assembly process to begin in 2-1/2 days. This reduces the starve/flood cycle by half. Continuing to decrease the batch size (and thus the cycle time of slitting) will result in one of two things happening. The feeding process of slitting is identified as the constraint, evidenced either by *no* product arriving early and the consistent starvation of downstream processes or by a buffer of product building up in front of the downstream processes, at which point the downstream constraint is identified as the bottleneck. After cutting the batches in half, we discovered that slitting was still starving the downstream processes. The downtime at assembly and shearing due to starvation was greatly diminished and total cycle time decreased, but starvation was still occurring. The next step was to examine remaining policies around how slitting was managed.

The second policy tackled was based on the same least-cost belief as batch sizes. In order to make the most efficient use of individual machine processes and ensure least-cost production, the slitting area had dedicated the large machines to producing the first cut from 4-foot wide rolls of woven material. The small slitters were then used to make a second cut, slitting the rolls into various widths. The large slitters were capable of producing the same final cuts as the small slitters but setup to do so required a full blade change, which took three times as long as adjusting the blade for different cuts on the small slitters. The long setup time at the large slitters fed the company belief that it was inefficient to use the large slitters from both a labor and a machine-utilization standpoint and would increase their unit cost. The large slitters sat idle 50% of the time, while downstream resources starved and on-time delivery hovered at 70%. This is an example of sticking to "best practice" or waiting until the resource perceived as being most cost effective is available, even though an acceptable alternative slitter is idle and could significantly increase throughput, reduce total cycle time, and increase cash flow and net profit without increasing operating expense. Breaking the policy around dedicating resources, maximizing batch sizes, and minimizing setups elevated the total capacity of slitting to the extent that it was no longer artificially the constrained area.

The setups at the large slitters were free. Breaking the two policy constraints, based on minimizing setup cost, immediately increased throughput, increased on-time delivery, decreased cycle time, increased net profit dramatically, and did *not* require any increase in spending for equipment, direct labor, or supplies. The belief that increasing process time at any operation increases the total product cost is *illogical*. If the operation has excess capacity, increasing time spent to process has no effect on the total cost. The decision to offload the constraint, the small slitters, to a process with excess capacity, even one with a longer process time, will result in a throughput increase for the entire plant, a total cycle-time reduction, and an elevation of the constraint with no capital equipment outlay. The concept of offloading the constraint resource and the true cost of setups are fully explored at the end of Chapter 5. Offloading the small slitters is analogous to Alex offloading items from Herbie's backpack and redistributing the weight among the other scouts in Goldratt's book, *The Goal*. The pace of the entire scout troop was dictated by Herbie's speed. Lightening Herbie's load allows the entire troop to move faster.

The examples are numerous, but the underlying cause remains the same. Any improvement process that ignores the need to focus and manage the constraining resource is *not* going to maximize profit. Any process improvement or program that hinders the constrained resource's ability to produce will have a debilitating effect on the financial health of the company. If the measures or key performance objectives are focused on local optimization of a non-constrained cost center, the actions taken to maximize the local measure or key performance indicator can show dramatic improvement, but the company can experience dramatic decreases in profitability. Policies, measures, and beliefs regarding efficient use of direct labor and machine utilization of both the non-constraints and the constraint are the consistent core problems in limiting capacity of the constraint process to improve throughput. All of the above stories were instances where the ability to exploit the constraint was limited by the policy, measure, or work practice used to manage either the resources feeding the constraint or the constraint resource itself.

One of my major frustrations in recent years has been the mindless adoption of viewing all inventory reductions as positive. Industry has swung to a new extreme that is detrimental to the bottom line. This simple view has led many companies to measure inventory at month end and reward or punish based on the objective of minimizing inventory at that one point. I have been in companies where the policy is to refuse to receive raw materials during the last five days of the month. The objective is to reduce inventory, to maximize inventory turn numbers, and to window dress their cash position. The results are that the production line is starved of materials and throughput declines. The plant plays catch-up over the rest of the month using expensive overtime and still misses customer ship dates. This policy puts the plant manager and the purchasing and inventory managers in direct conflict. Inventory turn numbers, using artificially depressed numbers at the month's end, do not give a true picture of the average inventory on hand throughout the year or the true inventory turns. This is an example of substituting a key performance indicator for the goal of the system. Another way of stating this is subordinating the organization to maximize a key performance indicator ignores the interdependencies of the system and results in suboptimization for the company as a whole.

Having the least amount of inventory in the system is the natural outcome of the following interdependent and necessary conditions:

1. Producing to order
2. Releasing material at the rate of the constraint or critical process
3. Reasonably buffering the constraint to ensure it is not starved
4. Maximizing the uptime of the constraint process
5. Purchasing to ensure a buffer of raw materials so the beginning process can start in time to maintain the constraint's buffer
6. Ensuring the reliability of all processes to support reasonable buffer levels in front of the critical processes

Be careful here! None of these actions can stand by themselves. All are necessary conditions. The key here is to understand the interdependencies among the above conditions. The conflict arises when one or two of the conditions becomes the focus for driving improvement methodology. The condition is translated into a "key performance indicator" and becomes the end objective of the improvement process. Can you think of any instances in your company when a key initiative actually hurt the ability of the company to perform its primary purpose of shipping product on time?

The above actions are also interdependent around ensuring the lowest cycle time — the least cash outflow and the highest rate of on-time delivery. The policy on not receiving raw material at the end of the month to drive down inventory valuation actually harms the ability of the company to increase inventory turns, deliver on time, reduce cycle time, and reduce costs. The negative effect is the result of ignoring interdependencies and confusing an intermediary effect with the goal of making money. Many companies have what I call the "great eight" or the "fabulous five" or the "sexy six" key business objectives or initiatives. Typically, these will include reduce costs, increase on-time delivery, increase inventory turns, improve quality, and gain market share. Each of you can easily think up actions, some of which perhaps your company has taken, that have individually driven one of the "fabulous five" up but invariably have driven the others in the opposite direction, including profit. The need to define the interrelationship of and prioritize company performance targets or objectives is the responsibility of top management. This concept and how to use the TOC thought process to accomplish prioritization are explored in length in Chapter 10.

The assignment of specific key objectives to mid-management creates even more conflict and dysfunction than standard cost accounting. Mid-managers fight for resources to maximize their performance objective, without considering or understanding the effect on the constrained process. Examples of the types of conflicts that materialize in the plant from these competing programs and performance objectives are diagrammed in Chapter 2 (Figure 2.2) using what I call the *spider web cloud of conflicts*, which is an example of the use of the thought-process tool called the *cloud* to logically diagram any conflicting situation. The process of using clouds to logically diagram the conflict traces the cause of the conflict to the programs and actions designed around maximizing different key objectives. Conflict arises when competing programs/objectives require that opposite actions be taken by a single person or department. On the one hand, the individual must take this action to be in compliance with the first program, but on the other they are also responsible for maintaining or implementing a second program and it requires a different or opposite action. I call these *competing measures*. Often the only course of action for the individual or department is to compromise both programs and ultimately the bottom line.

Without comprehensive education of mid-management and the ability to clearly diagram the conflict, middle management and first-line supervisors are hopelessly forced into action that usually compromises at least one of the objectives. If they are being measured with multiple competing objectives, they are set up to fail. Usually the plant performance is judged on the outcomes of all of the competing measures so it is impossible for the plant to win. It is still possible for the person in charge of only one program to "win" but often everyone else and the company loses.

Clearly, maximizing individual performance objectives violates step three of the Theory of Constraints: Subordinate everything else in the organization to the decision to exploit the constraint. Mastering step three, subordination, is the key to succeeding with TOC. Mastery of step three is dependent on a methodology of aligning measures, performance objectives, strategies, and policies to support maximizing return on investment. Return on investment is centered on understanding the interdependencies of the constraining resources and the rest of the organization. Creating a repeatable process with generic predictable effects that cross all organizational boundaries is no simple task. The difficulty is transferring a generic process to mid-management so they can extrapolate from the generic and create a robust, interactive solution for their environment. This solution must clearly link actions and outcomes to the interdependencies specific to the organization's constraint. By definition, environments are constantly changing so the solution must be a real-time and interactive process.

In order for the process to be transferable, it must be user friendly (easily understood and practical for day-to day use) and supported by upper management, and the manager must experience identifiable "wins" with the new process. Up until 1996, the thought-process tools were only offered in a two-week course commonly called the "Jonah" course. The participants in the research for my first book clearly expressed their dissatisfaction with the Jonah course as a user-friendly process. As powerful as the Jonah course was, the spread of TOC has been hindered by the long learning curve and the difficulty of transferring the process into day-to-day use inside companies. The newest iteration of the thought process is grounded in making the tools transferable and practical and is centered on what is being called the "day-to-day thought-process tools." I have used and further developed these day-to-day tools as the basis for defining and maintaining the new set of metrics necessary to maintain a TOC environment. Throughout the book, I have used cases from my clients to illustrate how these companies are redefining their environment and culture in order to adopt TOC as their framework for decision-making and management of the company. TOC is a framework and can be used to enhance all of the good tools a company has acquired by giving the company a way to focus their strengths and remove their resource contention conflicts.

Everyone has been looking for a set of measures that look like the old standard efficiency measures or the new key objective measures. My work has led me to conclude that measures cannot be predefined in a TOC environment. Because environments are constantly changing, the new metrics require the ability to examine what action is needed in the subordinating area based on knowing what outcome is desired to support the constraint. It is not a mindless set of "always take these actions" or "maximize a key performance indicator" — instead, it requires examining the existing environment, the barometer around the constraint. Based on the environment, the action is obvious because the outcome is a predictable effect based on a solid understanding of the interdependencies in the system.

The better a company becomes at the "right" response/interpretation cycle, the better the ability to subordinate and exploit. The day-to-day thought-process tool of the cloud, the logical diagram of conflict, has been one of the principal tools I have adapted to allow companies to create this response/ interpretation cycle.

The clouds clearly show when to take which action in order to maximize throughput and reduce cycle time. Clouds give people a method to examine the assumptions underlying the necessity for the action that they are proposing. Often the underlying assumptions predicating the need for the action are not valid in a specific instance. Exposing the assumptions around the proposed action gives an individual the ability to clearly communicate why the action is or is not desirable. Relating the assumptions to the state of the constraining resource clearly shows the workforce which action is necessary this time.

If a company is going to harness the focusing power of TOC, the organization must not only identify the key areas for managing throughput, but also must educate all supporting areas on to how evaluate their actions/measures and change their behavior to support exploitation of the constrained capacity resource. Continuously solving the causes of starvation or downtime at the constraint creates a continuous improvement cycle. Without the ability to cause all other resources to subordinate to support the constrained resource, a company will be unable to exploit the constraint and therefore unable to exploit their investment to achieve the highest return. Chapters 5, 6, and 7 explain the basis for a feedback and measurement system for the TOC production solution, Drum-Buffer-Rope, and the details of how to create real-time subordination measures and methods.

2 The Measurement Nightmare

The basic theory in throughput accounting and Drum-Buffer-Rope (DBR) scheduling mirrors the direct costing and incremental or relevant costing taught in any beginning management accounting course. The philosophy of exploiting the drum is the part of the practice surrounding the same principle expressed in every management accounting text regarding profit maximization. The following excerpt is taken from one of the most popular management accounting texts in use in universities today (*Introduction to Management Accounting*, 9th ed., by Horngren et al., Prentice Hall, New York, 1993). It is common core curriculum for management accounting and is covered in similar verbiage in all introductory texts.

> *The criterion for maximizing profits when one factor limits sales is to obtain the greatest possible contribution to profit for each unit of the limiting or scarce factor. The product that is most profitable when one particular factor limits sales may be the least profitable if a different factor restricts sales. When there are limitations, the conventional contribution or gross margin-per-sales-dollar ratios provide an insufficient clue to profitability.*

Exploiting the scarce resource exploits the investment of the whole organization. The existence of a limiting resource negates the validity of conventional contribution or gross margin analysis. I am going to take the concept one step further: *The existence of a limiting factor makes the conventional process of relevant costing or the conventional process of selecting relevant information insufficient unless the relevant costs or data are considered in light of the constraining resource.* The framework I have taught companies to use is the same process I use to challenge my own or any system's logic regarding the relevancy of data or information in the current environment. This framework is my most valuable tool; it is the method for logically diagramming conflict known as the *cloud.* The cloud is a framework designed to challenge the logic around different potential courses of action based on understanding why the actions are necessary to protect the necessary conditions of the system.

The definition of relevant information from the *Introduction to Management Accounting* follows:

> *We emphasize the purpose of management accounting is to provide information that enable managers to make sound decisions. The focus is identifying relevant information for particular management decisions. ...What information is relevant depends on the decision being made. Decision-making is essentially choosing among several courses of action. The available actions are determined by an often time-consuming formal or informal search and screening process, perhaps carried on by a company team that includes engineers, accountants, and operating executives. In the final stages of the decision-making process, managers compare two or more alternative courses of action. The decision is based on the difference in the effect of each alternative on future performance. Relevant information is the predicted future costs and revenues that will differ among alternatives.*

The existence of a limiting factor changes the basic assumptions underlying the cost and revenue opportunity of a potential action. This fundamental concept is the basis of my work with companies. Making a practical bridge allows them to align their strategies with local actions and measures and make the best decisions as to how to maximize the return on their given set of resources in both the short and long run.

The complexity of the product cost systems varies from company to company, with an increasing trend to more and more complicated allocation systems, often driven by some form of activity-based costing. The accounting figures generated are a mixture of current costs and historical costs adjusted on the basis of a future estimate of asset useful life. At best, they involve judgment; at worst, massaging based on manipulation of current reported profit. The decision to base incentives or reward systems on traditional reported net profit results is a dysfunctional management decision. *At no time do these traditional systems consider the two basic premises of management accounting: management of the scarce resource and using relevant information to choose action alternatives.*

In many cases decisions are made in earnest attempts to maximize short-run company performance, but, with the erroneous allocations reflected in the product costing and profit reporting, poor decisions by companies reflect the quality of the information used to make them. More importantly, the information generated is used to report standard cost variances for raw materials purchase price and usage, machine-utilization efficiencies, direct labor costs, and usage variances at each stage of production. These local efficiencies drive action on the production floor and in the departments supporting production into dysfunctional behavior. The measures become the driving force behind the actions taken — from the purchase of materials, to the batching of orders, to the priority of maintenance, tooling, and equipment acquisition.

Maximizing local efficiencies creates an inherent conflict between departments and places the production manager in a basic internal conflict verbalized as follows: In order to ship on time, the constrained resource must be exploited and the operation managed as a chain of events. All resources must run at the pace of the constraint. In order to minimize unit product cost, all resources must run at maximum efficiency. Shipping on time and minimizing unit costs are the necessary conditions for being a good production manager and are the criteria on which the production manager's job performance is evaluated. *Fulfilling these criteria, however, requires two different actions that are in direct conflict with each other.*

In order to exploit the constrained resource and manage the operation as a chain of events, the manager must pace raw material release to the pace of the constraint. Any operation outpacing the constraining resource only adds to expenses and inventory without contributing to the throughput of the company. This pacing action will result in low labor efficiencies at the non-constrained resources.

In a traditional costing environment, in order to produce a least-cost unit, *all* production resources must maximize their output and run at maximum efficiency. This will increase overtime and work-in-process and raw material inventories and lengthen the cycle time. Clearly, these are opposite actions with opposite results. No wonder floor managers are confused and constantly fight fires. It is the logical culmination of compromising between maximizing local utilization and effectively moving product through the plant.

Look at this conflict in the form of the thought-process tool called a *cloud*. The cloud provides a simple method of logically diagramming conflict. The conflict stated above is represented in Figure 2.1. The top and the bottom of the cloud are read separately, starting with the plant manager's objective (A), followed by the necessary condition to fulfill the objective (B), then the specific action required to achieve the necessary condition (D). The top of the cloud would be read in the following manner: To meet the objective of maximizing operations performance measures (A), the plant must ship on time (B). To maximize shipping on time, all resources must operate at the pace of the constraining resource (D). The assumption connecting B to D is that managing the constrained resource will maximize the throughput in the shortest cycle time.

The sequence is repeated on the bottom: To meet the objective of maximizing operations performance measures (A), the plant must produce parts at the least cost (C). In order to produce parts at the least cost per unit, all resources must operate at maximum efficiency (D'). The assumption connecting C to D' is that maximizing local optima will minimize global cost. This assumption is

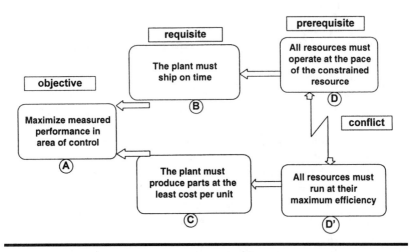

Figure 2.1. Operations Conflict Using Standard Accounting (©Eli Goldratt)

flawed and is the source of tremendous waste and extra cost. If the plant cannot create throughput faster than the constraining resource, maximizing output at other resources simply creates extra work-in-process inventory on the floor, increasing cycle time and decreasing cash flow.

This basic generic conflict stated above has many verbalizations at local levels in operations. The following are common conflict examples caused by standard cost-variance analysis (or a mentality of least-cost parts) and common-sense plant operations. The multiple cloud format shows how noisy and conflict-laden the typical manufacturing environment can become. Eight common measurement clouds are presented in Figure 2.2. I named the least-cost part *spider web*. Read the clouds individually and compare them to your operations. Do these measurements require actions that conflict with each other?

An example of how to read the diagram of conflicts is demonstrated by using the middle lower cloud with the two conflicting actions of building to order and building to stock. To read a cloud, start with the common objective in the middle of the diagram: To be a responsible manager, I must respond to the market; to respond to the market, I must build to order. On the other hand, to be a responsible manager, I must also maximize labor and machine efficiency; to maximize labor and machine efficiency I must build to stock. I cannot both build to stock and build to order; hence, managers compromise both of the necessary conditions by trying to do some form of both. Read the rest of the conflicts and see how they fit with your experience.

These conflicts are common in every environment to which I have been exposed. In fact, they are so common they are not even questioned. People have given up. Both sides of the cloud make logical sense to everyone and this is how we (and everybody else) operate. It is common practice, *not* common sense.

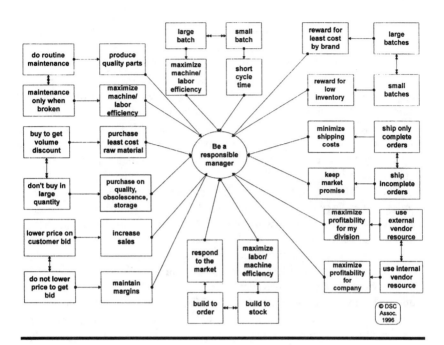

Figure 2.2. Spider Web Conflict Cloud

The Avraham Y. Goldratt Institute (AGI) defines a chronic conflict as one so embedded in our lives that we have accepted the conflict as irreconcilable and are constantly compromising by choosing which side of the cloud we will act on today.

How did we end up in the nightmare where intelligent, hardworking people are trapped in chronic conflicts that they cannot accurately define, let alone resolve? More importantly, why is the logical process of accounting producing such illogical results and demanding conflicting actions from people? Worse yet, managers commonly try to manage their resources by compromising both objectives. This results in the total chaos that characterizes manufacturing floors of today.

Ultimately, this leads to total confusion for the workforce. Any sane person resents taking actions that are in direct conflict with their common sense. This is the underlying reason for the common belief by labor that management either does not understand their jobs or they are just blatantly stupid. One easy way to block throughput and make less money is to confuse the people doing the work.

In my early consulting days I once spoke with a woman in production and asked her what the problems in her area were and what changes she would recommend. She gave me several excellent ideas. I asked her if she had mentioned these to her boss. She looked at me skeptically and replied she wasn't paid to think, all thinking was left to management. I asked her how she identified someone as being in management, and she pointed out that all managers had the distinctive feature of wearing neckties; she also added that I, as a female, was obviously exempt from thinking. She then winked at me and told me her theory correlating neckties and brain damage. I have often thought of her when I am showing companies the obvious conflicts in their reporting and measuring metrics. I have come to the conclusion that it is not the neckties but the flawed assumptions driving their measurements that cause the brain damage. When we are constantly placed in situations that require firefighting actions, the result is we light tomorrow's fires.

The initial reaction from operations people and even presidents of companies is that "Accounting is out of our hands. It is technical and we don't know how or why they do what they do." This is true to the extent that we cannot change the requirements of generally accepted accounting principles (GAAP), but we can change our internal management accounting practice and use relevant information to make good decisions.

I have heard many executives make the statement, "We don't let accounting run our business." *They are dead wrong!* They are letting outdated accounting numbers and standard costing techniques, such as local efficiency measures, run their business, and they are unwitting accomplices. The four basic decisions made by every company are commonly reached using standard accounting cost information rather than direct costing and incremental cash flow. Even with cash-flow decisions, companies fail to use a constrained resource focus that would allow the organization to prioritze actions around the effect on the constraining resource. These four decisions are

1. Product emphasis
2. Product pricing
3. Capital-investment and process-improvement expenditures
4. Addition of a product or market niche and deletion of a product or business segment

Chapter 9 examines the fundamental flawed assumptions all businesses make when analyzing the above decisions. Use this chapter to examine how your own company makes decisions vs. how they would be made in a management accounting approach with a TOC focus to determine relevant costing information.

Here is a simple example to which every person who has been exposed to standard cost-variance analysis can relate. The purchase price variance is a highly visible variance reported from the top to the bottom and often is reported as a line item in the financial statements. Every effort is made by the purchasing department to have a favorable variance, to purchase at a cost less than the standard cost assigned for raw materials. Knowing this, a purchasing manager has found a very good buy on wood for their wood-products milling division and has made a large-lot purchase (4 months of materials). The purchase price variance is very large, and, in accordance with GAAP, the entire variance is recorded at the time of the purchase, favorably impacting the financial statements in the month the purchase is received. For the next 4 months, the plant performance is directly related to the quality of the wood purchased, and unfortunately the quality is substandard; the wood has twice the "normal" amount of knotholes per board foot.

The direct labor variance is unfavorable for both labor hours and labor rate because overtime increases significantly throughout the plant as operations spend time cutting out the knotholes and wood imperfections. Slowdowns are passed on to every station. The bottleneck is starved, and subsequent operations work overtime to catch up. Shipments are late, and on-time delivery performance deteriorates. The raw material usage variance is unfavorable, and scrap rates are high. All of the unfavorable variances are passed on to the operations measures. The worst case is the purchasing manager is promoted, and the plant manager is fired. The best case is we can connect one department's overtime and the increased scrap to the substandard purchase but we do not link the rest of the plant's increased cost, throughput loss, and potential market loss from missed shipments to the purchase decision. This is just one example of a local area maximizing its efficiency metric at the expense of the global good.

Imagine the power of an organization that can easily make the effect-cause-effect links to the above situation, change its measures and actions, and communicate the necessity for change both up and down the organization.

The fact that cost accounting fails to make a lot of sense is not new news. Since *Relevance Lost* was published in 1980, cost accountants have been bashed, but very little has been done to change the basic premise of cost accounting. Every attempt at innovation ends up looking like the same old solution and causing the same problems as standard cost accounting. The underlying cause of the above measurement and the solution to the conflict have taken me 8 years to document and can be stated in a logical diagram I call the accounting dilemma (Figure 2.3).

The objective of accounting (A) is to satisfy the informational needs of all the stakeholders of a business, both external and internal:

1. To satisfy *all* stakeholder requirements (A), the company must comply with the reporting requirements of the Internal Revenue Service, Securities and Exchange Commission, investors, creditors, and other regulatory agencies (B). To meet those requirements, companies must compile financial reporting according to GAAP (D).

2. To satisfy *all* stakeholders requirement (A), the company must generate information to make good business decisions internally (C). To make good decisions internally, the company must use throughput accounting/radical direct-costing accounting information (D').

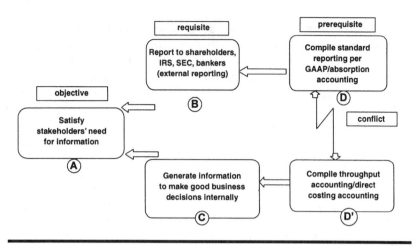

Figure 2.3. Evaporating Cloud: Identify Conflict Preventing TOC Accounting Integration in Financial Reporting and Information

To analyze a logical diagram it is necessary to examine the underlying assumptions that influence and glue the logic together. The fundamental logic of GAAP is beyond my scope to credit or discredit. Chapter 4 is a short explanation of four of the basic rules of GAAP that result in product costing and standard cost-variance analysis. It is essential reading for anyone who is gauged or measured on standard product unit cost and is trying to make sense of it. Chapter 4 attempts to make a simple and coherent explanation of the basic issues in product costing, under GAAP reporting. Suffice it to say that compliance with GAAP is a necessary condition of doing business in the U.S.

Chapters 1 and 2 should have sufficiently convinced you of the need for new operational performance measures and accounting management information to encourage and sustain performance improvement processes aimed at reducing cycle time and inventory and improving quality. If you agree we must conform to reporting requirements and we must change how we measure and reward in managed organizations, then you understand clearly the following statement: *Both GAAP compliance and throughput accounting are necessary conditions for companies to do business successfully. If both are necessary, why don't we have both?*

If we need both, but cannot seem to provide both at the same time, the solution is probably hidden in one of the basic assumptions about why they cannot both exist. By asking the following question we can examine and challenge the assumptions at the conflict arrow between (D) and (D'): Why must we only have either a GAAP accounting system or a throughput system in place? Why can't we have both? In analyzing our accounting cloud, the common assumptions given as to why we can only have one or the other are

1. Absorption and throughput accounting are not easily reconciled.
2. The company cannot afford two systems.
3. The system is already too complex to add anything new.
4. There is no bridge for the management accounting theory of "profit maximization through the management of the limited resource" to practical application and relevant information generation.
5. Our training/experience/system is all in absorption accounting. We do not know how!

The solution to this problem is the purpose of this book. Chapter 8 explains, through a simple example, the standard method of reconciling both direct and absorption costing and addresses the first and second assumptions. The reconciliation process is not new or even innovative; every small accounting firm, with cash-basis clients, performs this exercise at least on an annual basis, and most computer systems can easily perform the basics of both. The rest of the book is devoted to the fourth assumption and provides new concepts. By addressing the first four assumptions, we can remove them and empower you, the reader, with the ability to remove the fifth assumption. Chapters 6 and 7 explain how accepted management accounting solutions, direct costing, relevant costing, and opportunity costing fit new operations methods such as Drum-Buffer-Rope and Just-in-Time. Re-discovering management accounting, through a logical effect-cause-effect framework, validates how we can, and why we need to, make operations decisions and design measures to drive actions that are aligned with the strategic objectives of the company and maximize return on investment. This is a win-win situation for all of the stakeholders, externally and internally.

3 Theory of Constraints: The Evolution of a Revolution

The core idea in the Theory of Constraints (TOC) is that every real system, such as a profit-making company, must have at least one constraint. If this were not true, then the system would produce an infinite amount of whatever it strives for; in the case of a constraint in a manufacturing company, it would be infinite profits. Because a constraint is a factor that limits the company from reaping more profits, then a business manager who wants more profit must manage constraints. There really is no choice in the matter. Either you manage the constraints or they manage you. The constraints will determine the throughput of the system whether they are acknowledged and managed or not; therefore, managing the constraints determines the rate of return on the investment a company will experience.

The Theory of Constraints simplifies managing a complex environment if the environment can be optimally managed around a few constraining resources. Instead of managing the dependencies of every event and every resource to every other event and resource, all resources manage their events around a few constraining resources. The simplicity of the system is the ability to monitor and leverage a few key points in the operations flow. The clarity gained from understanding the role of the constraining resource allows a company to see the environment without confusion resulting from all the noise inherent in any complex system.

It is the noise in the system that stops us from understanding how to create simple solutions focused around the system leverage points, the limited resources. Instead, managers and workers are constantly battling the symptoms with very little results. The beauty of TOC is that it simplifies a complex environment to the point that it can be understood, aligned, and managed. TOC creates the bridge to focus and define the criteria for relevant information to evaluate clearly and choose among the best of multiple alternatives.

Any business can be viewed as a linked sequence of processes that transform some input into a sellable product. In TOC, an analogy often is drawn between such a system and a chain. If you want to improve the strength of the chain, what is the most effective way to do it? Do you concentrate on strengthening the strongest link? Do you concentrate on strengthening the largest link? Do you apply your efforts uniformly over all the links? Or, should you attempt to identify the weakest link and then concentrate your efforts on strengthening that single link? Clearly, the last course will return the biggest benefit in relation to the effort expended.

The procedure to follow in strengthening is straightforward:

1. Identify the weakest link, which is the constraint. Identifying it may not be easy, because most businesses attempt to cope with fluctuating demands and random disruption by maintaining buffer inventories at each step of the process. These work-in-process inventories hide problems, obscure interdependencies, and make it difficult to identify the real constraint in the system.
2. Do not try to subject the system to too great a load. If a larger load is placed on the chain than the weakest link can handle, the chain will break. The weakest link should set the pace for the entire system.
3. Concentrate improvement efforts on the weakest link.
4. If the improvement efforts are successful, eventually the weakest link will improve to the point where it is no longer the weakest link. Any further efforts to improve the former weakest link will provide little or no benefit. At this point, the new weakest link must be identified, and the improvement efforts must be shifted over to that link.

This sequential process focuses resources where they will do the most good and is the basis for continuous improvement. The TOC approach to continuous improvement is a perfect complement to Total Quality Management (TQM). TOC gives management the ability to focus TQM efforts on the points in the organization where they are most effective. Currently, TOC comprises three major groups of techniques. The first group encompasses generic solutions designed to deal with managing physical production (an in-depth explanation of the production solution is provided in Chapter 5), distribution, and project management constraints or external constraints such as the market or vendor relationships. The second group consists of the generic problem-solving tool known as the *thinking process*, which is a logic framework designed to facilitate breakthrough solutions for an organization (for a detailed update on thought-process changes, see the Appendix). The third group includes the day-to-day thought-process tools and specific uses of the thought-process tools designed to deal with improving everyday communication, initiating skills, empowerment skills, and team-building skills. The production, distribution, project management, and external constraints solutions and the day-to-day thought-process tools are specific applications of the logic-based thought process. They are about being able to successfully define and solve conflicts with focus and a repeatable process.

Eli Goldratt first became interested in business because of the problems associated with scheduling production, but he quickly realized that improving scheduling would have limited benefits. Further, sustained improvements would depend on how the constraints of the process were managed. His first book, *The Goal*, was the product of his production scheduling thinking and concentrates on managing production constraints. The techniques illustrated in *The Goal*, such as Drum-Buffer-Rope (DBR) scheduling and the five steps for continuous improvement through focusing on the constraints, can be applied quickly and easily to capacity-constrained job shops with high product diversity. Applying these techniques has consistently resulted in immediate payoff in terms of greater throughput, improved due-date performance, reduced cycle-time performance, improved quality statistics, decreased inventory, and increased cash flow.

In research sponsored by the Institute of Management Accounting that studied 21 companies in both Europe and North America, we found this payoff to be the case in nearly all of the companies examined. Numerous independent studies have substantiated the quick and relatively painless superiority of TOC to Just-in-Time (JIT) as a process of ongoing improvement to manage production. Drum-Buffer-Rope has become so well documented and accepted that it has earned a place in several of the most popular operations management books currently being used at major universities across the country. Even APICS has adopted TOC and has just hosted the third annual, national convention featuring only TOC.

Unfortunately, because of the way *The Goal* was written, TOC was generally pigeon-holed as a "manufacturing thing" relevant only in a job shop that is having difficulty meeting due dates. This impression is incorrect. TOC is a broad-based management strategy tool that has been successfully applied to specific situations, such as production scheduling, distribution, project management, and marketing, but, more importantly, it is a repeatable, proven process to solve chronic problems by surfacing breakthrough solutions. The thought-process methods were developed after the methods for dealing with physical production bottlenecks were developed. Goldratt codified how he arrived at his production solution, and the thinking processes were born. Goldratt applied the discipline and concepts from managing a system in physics to managing a system in business.

The day-to-day thought-process tools are the latest TOC tool development and were specifically developed using the thought process to address the problems associated with developing and communicating the culture change necessary for successful implementation of TOC to the workforce and management. The major part of my work has centered on developing and using the day-to-day thought process tools to develop measurement, policy, and strategy alignment around constraint management. These tools are the practical bridge between TOC and generating relevant information for management decisions to maximize return on investment (ROI). The use of the day-to-day tools is how I help an organization to identify and change current policies, work practices, and measures that conflict with their decision to manage their constraints. The tools are practical and powerful and can be used to align ROI with local actions and measures. Most importantly, they are practicable across the organization. Anyone can learn them in a few days!

The first evolution of TOC, brought about by the initial popularity of *The Goal*, resulted in successfully shifting the bottleneck outside of the factory. At that point, further improvements were often stymied because managers outside of production had not been exposed to TOC or did not see the relevance of TOC. They lacked the ability to adapt the principles of TOC to the organization as a whole. The company was often unable to convert the excess production capacity exposed from the plant's improvement to sales in the marketplace. If a company was unable to sell its improvements in the marketplace, the only way to improve the bottom-line performance was to revert to cutting costs. Unfortunately, the area most able to sustain a reduction in headcount was also the area that had improved the most — production. This stopped improvement in the factory and led to a loss of morale and significant distrust on the part of the workforce for any improvement processes. In some cases, organizations regressed severely. This situation is one of the potential pitfalls of improperly implementing TOC which any potential adopter should be aware of.

These difficulties led Goldratt to the development of a generic approach for diagnosing and solving problems — the thinking process (TP). The principles laid out in *The Goal* are simply examples of the application of the TP to a particular set of problems generic to the production floor. Using the TP, the Theory of Constraints is no longer inappropriately confined to the shop floor. The generic TP approach involves building logical trees, which basically are cause-and-effect diagrams. Starting with observed symptoms of problems, cause-and-effect reasoning is used to deduce underlying causes, or core problems. Other logical trees are then used to identify and refine solutions and construct step-by-step implementation plans.

When first designed and taught, in the early 1990s, the process was complex and difficult to master. Using the generic thought processes proved too expensive and unwieldy as the only means of transferring knowledge to a company. The "Jonah" course, a two-week crash course in TPs, was the primary means for accomplishing the knowledge transfer and culture shift required to implementing TOC successfully. The companies that used the full power of TOC consistently reported impressive gains in financial results and in key operating statistics such as cycle time and due-date performance but generally felt they were leaving a large potential untapped. The general consensus of managers at the sites we visited during research for our first book was dissatisfaction with how much TOC they had put into practice. They were happy with what they had accomplished but usually thought that they should have done more and were hampered by lack of time or a lack of confidence and skills to use the TPs. Today's evolution of the "Jonah" TP is much simpler and more powerful. An updated explanation of the "new" TP techniques is presented in the Appendix.

Consistently, erroneous measures, policies, and work practices caused unresolved chronic conflicts in the organizations we visited. These measures failed to reflect interdependencies of the key objectives of the organization and were in almost all instances tied to standard cost accounting or local efficiency measures or work practices. The constant firefighting necessary to manage a non-aligned organization left managers little time to focus on real system improvement. The spider web of conflicts shown in Chapter 2 (Figure 2.2) uses eight real examples of the conflicts managers confront daily.

As often stated in the TQM and JIT literature, as well as in TOC literature, the success of any program that involves a major cultural change in an organization depends on the involvement of top management. At sites where top management did not view the business from a TOC perspective, there were usually problems. The biggest problems were with top managers who continued to evaluate production and market managers based on measures of efficiency and cost accounting gross profit figures by product rather than profits on throughput dollars. It is impossible to divorce TOC operations from TOC accounting and measures. Any attempt to run a TOC operation while using traditional management accounting measures, controls, and incentives is doomed to failure. Integral to the new measurement system is the need to create a total shift away from the ingrained "cost/efficiency" mentality. Unless this is done, the company will continue to send conflicting signals and take conflicting action.

To solve the core problem of local measures causing chronic conflicts among departments, thought-process tools were adapted for everyday problem solving. This TP application has been dubbed the *day-to-day thought-process tools*. It is the third and the most recent evolution in the TOC product offerings. The tools provide any level of employee with the ability to significantly improve their communication skills, initiating skills, empowerment skills, and team skills.

The innovation of creating simpler tools addresses the dissatisfaction expressed by managers over their own or their employees' abilities to disseminate and implement TOC principles quickly and successfully. I have solved this problem by integrating both the TOC production solution and the use of day-to-day thought-process tools into a tool set that allows people to challenge their measures and work practices at all levels in the organization. People are taught to base the solution around making the best decisions to maximize performance of the constraining resources the company has identified as critical to generating throughput. Previously, large companies have had extreme difficulty sustaining a TOC environment. My experience demonstrates the approach is sound for both small and large companies.

Small companies, although lacking sophisticated standard cost accounting systems, are still firmly entrenched in the mindset of parts per man-hour or machine-hour. Repeatedly, I have heard, "Cost accounting is not a problem here." My response is, "What do machine operators or floor supervisors routinely concentrate on to measure their performance?" The answer is always some form of efficiencies at their individual workstation. The optimization of local performance is always the focal point of an individual efficiency measure and leads to the same dysfunctional behavior as large companies with sophisticated costing systems. *It is not the degree of sophistication of the costing system that causes the conflict but the ingrained and pervasive local cost world mentality, regardless of size or sophistication.*

My experience in manufacturing led me to the following hypothesis and my research confirmed it: *Current measurement practice and incentive and reward programs lead to the majority of conflict and result in dysfunctional behavior across the organization.* Unless the standard cost measurement mindset and reporting structure can be defused to allow separation of management information for decision-making (both strategic and day-to-day operations) from financial accounting information for external reporting purposes, managers will be torn between two conflicting priorities: "Do what is best for the organization as a whole (maximize throughput and cash flow), or do what is best to maximize the local area performance measurement (maximize my area efficiency measures)." This is the local cost world vs. the throughput world dilemma.

The conflict inherent in this performance measurement has two components. The first aspect of the dilemma is the internal conflict experienced by employees if they are aware that their actions are dysfunctional to the organization as a whole. I firmly believe, after talking to hundreds of people at all organizational levels across numerous companies, that employees intuitively understand the conflict between what they are measured on, or told to do, and what makes sense to move product through the plant. They *believe* that maximizing output through their area is good, yet they live with and constantly battle the conflict that their actions cause if their area is not the constraint. Increased cycle time, increased work in process, increased handling, increased expediting, and increased quality failures are associated with long runs and large batch sizes. Employees firefight the results but cannot clearly articulate the effect-cause-effect relationship, and they see no alternatives to compromising between maximizing their individual output and trying to expedite product to ship on time. Managers and workers are truly stuck in this chronic conflict.

The second aspect of the dilemma is the external conflict which finds employees or departments pitted against each other. This is compounded in companies that have gone to the "mini-company" management concept that is prevalent in the automotive industry. This concept makes profit centers out of every department in production. Quite literally it becomes a matter of "screw your buddy" or move the problem downstream. Managers hoard resources, rely on quality failures to be exposed somewhere else, and fight for scarce tooling and maintenance time. My first experiment with combining day-to-day thought-process tools and production application with my measurement workshops was with a company firmly entrenched in this profit-center philosophy.

Working with this company showed me the true power of the TP tool, the cloud, to expose chronic measurement conflicts in an organization. I had the opportunity to teach the day-to-day thought-process tools to 24 supervisors and managers at all levels of the company. On the third day of this training, I asked each participant to pick a dispute or conflict they were involved in with another area or manager in the company. The only two criteria were that:

1. Each person must want to solve the conflict.
2. The other person or department must be aware of the conflict.

Within 3 hours, the entire group shifted from their original position of what they had perceived as being conflict to understanding the core underlying issues that the diagrammed conflict exposed. The power of the cloud clearly lies in its ability to expose both sides of the conflict. The cloud made the following overwhelmingly clear:

1. The people or areas they were in conflict with were trying to protect very real needs of their own and the system; they were not simply trying to thwart the other people.
2. Identifying why we want what we are fighting for forces us to take a deep look at the real reason we are in conflict. This is a very powerful tool for understanding our own motivation, and it is amazing how difficult it is for us to logically link why what we want is essential to what we need to do our job.
3. The real conflict was not with the other employees or departments but with a policy or measure each was trying to follow or maximize in their areas. Why the conflict exists was exposed, as well as the common objective each side was trying to protect.
4. Exposing the needs of both sides as being linked logically to a common objective allowed each side to understand and defuse the negative emotion that had developed in regard to the others.
5. In half of the instances, even with both sides in agreement, they could not solve the conflict. If both sides were trying to enforce a policy or maximize a measure in their own areas, clearly the only way to remove the conflict was to break the policies or remove the measures. In most cases, the parties at odds did not have the authority to do either.

6. Exposing the flawed measures, policies, and work practices is one of the fastest and most inexpensive ways to get an instant throughput improvement.

The attitude was no longer one of "me against you"; instead, it changed to "us against the cause of our conflict". This thought-process shift allows people to combine their efforts and to communicate to the policymaker why the policy or measure is dysfunctional. Better yet, employees can work together to construct a solution, new measure, policy, or work practice that protects the common objective of both the employees and the company. The beauty of clouds lies in their simplicity. Anyone can construct them, read them, and understand them in a very short period. I use clouds to expose erroneous policies and measures and competing actions that limit a company's ability to subordinate to the decision to exploit their constrained resource and maximize profit.

It is critical to forewarn top management that they will be the focal point for the frustration the conflict has caused once the source is identified as a conflicting policy or measure. Obviously, who ever set up the measures and policies is to blame. The only way to solve this problem is for top management to agree that the policy or measure is flawed. The attitude necessary to adopt TOC successfully must be that no policies are sacred. Management, by agreeing to sponsor TOC and specifically the day-to-day thought-process tools, is giving employees the tools to identify flawed policies and measures and to design appropriate measures to support the process of ongoing improvement. The employees become responsible for carrying out the actions necessary to subordinate to and exploit the constraint and are jointly responsible for identifying how their performance will be measured. The participants discover that identifying the "right" action requires understanding the interdependencies of their areas' actions on the ability of the constraint to perform.

Top management should understand the degree to which adopting TOC will challenge company management practices. If a company truly wants an empowered workforce, they are about to get one! The employees understand there is no place left to hide or someone else to blame. *They* are the *we*. Team building can truly begin with the recognition of shared responsibility across the board for policies and measures designed to ensure the common objective of maximizing throughput, which is an amazing change to accomplish in one day. I would doubt even the possibility of such an occurrence if I had not repeatedly participated in the process.

The next step is to design and implement measures and policies that tie local actions to the company's global goal without creating conflict. Critical to assessing the new measure or any new policy or idea is the ability of the group to evaluate or criticize without attacking the inventor. The day-to-day thought-process tools that evaluate proposed new policies and measures use the TP tool known as a *negative branch*, which logically diagrams the effect-cause-effect relationship of implementing a new idea to the potential pitfalls the idea could cause. The premise is that all good ideas lead to predictable negative consequences, some of which are not trivial. The use of the tool causes the inventor to see the logical link between the idea and the pitfall and the consequences of not dealing with the predicted outcome before implementation.

When a proposed idea or new solution is presented to a cross-functional team, there is a high probability someone will see an aspect that will cause problems, if not outright failure. Exposing the potential pitfalls allows the idea to be perfected before it is implemented or withdrawn altogether. Besides the obvious benefits of creating a more complete solution, the negative branch offers a way to criticize a new idea without offending the inventor. In fact, Eli Goldratt maintains that people have ceased offering new ideas because the common reaction is to attack the idea and focus in on the potential negatives, and the inventor feels attacked. Often these attacks or negative outcomes cannot be logically connected to the idea at all. A structured, simple method of dealing with criticism (the negative branch) that highlights the positive attributes of the idea and logically points out the potential negatives is a solid win for the whole team.

The possibility of a good solution that addresses all the potential negative ramifications increases with the breadth of the team building the negative branch. Correctly building and communicating a negative branch allows the inventor to properly address the negative concerns or ramifications without retreating to a defensive posture. Negative branches clarify the reservations logically and concisely explain the step-by-step causality. They systematically focus attention on solutions that have gone "bad" and the entry point necessary for another solution. More importantly, they do not sound like whining or a "can't-do" attitude. This is especially important if the inventor of the idea/solution is the boss.

The third day-to-day tool that has proved critical to breaking through the change barrier is a tool designed to address creation of a motivated team capable of implementing the changes in their environment, necessary for adopting new ideas and solutions. The tool known as a *prerequisite tree* is a time-sequenced road map that leads the team from the current old environment into the new solution environment. In order for each member of a team to fully commit his or her time and energy to the proposed solution, the following must be accomplished:

1. Each team member's concerns regarding the obstacles to the implementation must be acknowledged by the rest of the team.
2. The team must agree upon the resources necessary to overcome the obstacles blocking the implementation.
3. The specific assignment of who, what, and when must be correctly ordered or time sequenced. Time is wasted if resources are focused on obstacles that are dependent on the completion of other obstacles.

4. Resource contention inside the implementation or with competing project implementations must be identified and prioritized. Teams can use prerequisite trees to ask top management to prioritize projects that are competing for the same resource inside the organization. If prioritization is not made and the resource begins multi-tasking, both projects are delayed.
5. The prerequisite tree must be agreed upon as the method of measuring and reporting the progress of the implementation.
6. The prerequisite tree is a living document; undiscovered obstacles surfaced during the implementation must be added to the tree and addressed in sequence. The prerequisite tree is not finished until the objective is accomplished.

This tool is invaluable in generating consensus on direction and strategic alignment. It can be use with top management to clearly show them the alignment of multiple key strategic thrusts, and then each of the strategic thrusts can be handed down through the organization in smaller increments until the actual action plan to cause the change is at the lowest unit. The power of this is incredible. How many strategies are implemented, down to the local level, and remain aligned with the intent of the strategic vision from the top? My experience is very few. In addition, prerequisite trees align across functions and, by definition, acknowledge cross-function interdependencies of the strategy in the implementation.

Prerequisite trees also solve the dilemma of what to objectively measure a team's performance against. The prerequisite tree is created by the team and defines the team's resource requirements and time commitments. It is easy to see where the project is, who is responsible for the next step, and what remains to be completed. The team's creation of the prerequisite tree is critical to generating ownership in both the project and their ability to accomplish the project. People are unwilling to participate in a plan they believe has a high chance of failure. Their unwillingness to be associated with failure or their decision to put their efforts into something else with a better chance of success results in dooming the project at the beginning. People believe failure is inherent if they do not have faith in their teammates' ability to execute the plan or they do not believe the necessary resources will be dedicated to overcoming the obstacles they see to the implementation. Prerequisite trees address precisely these issues.

The ability to use the day-to-day tools and apply them to implementing Drum-Buffer-Rope scheduling solves many of the implementation issues and leads naturally to designing operational measures and reconciling accounting issues that will come up. They are the basis for exposing the interdependencies of key objectives and allowing management to prioritize the resource contentions that exist in every dynamic environment. These tools are the basis that enables me to transfer a dynamic implementation with a robust, maintainable cycle of improvement to my clients. Without a practical, user-friendly way to identify, communicate, and create solutions for conflict, any change process will fail. These tools can be used successfully in any environment.

Change exposes the conflicts that the environment has accepted as being *status quo*. Changing the *status quo* requires the ability to solve the conflicts the organization has avoided addressing in their current environment. An organization's unresolved conflicts define the effectiveness of the organization. An organization will remain in the stranglehold of the behavior patterns that their management beliefs, measures, work practice, and culture have defined as necessary conditions to survive in the organization, unless it can systematically expose and redefine them.

The purpose for writing about the evolution of TOC is to provide some insight into the "process" component of the thought process, which has been used for continuous improvement and expansion of the knowledge base and product offerings around constraint management.

4 How We Got into this Accounting Measuring Mess

O ne of the most blatant and public examples of earnings manipulation is the 1996 bonuses paid to Apple executives. After three consecutive losing quarters, Apple showed a third-quarter 1996 profit of $25 million. The following excerpt is from CNNfn from February 5, 1997:

> *Apple Computer Chairman, Gilbert Amelio, told the annual shareholders' meeting Wednesday that he was suspending Apple's executive cash bonus plan until the struggling computer maker returned to profitability. ...Amelio's comments came a day after the company announced another restructuring and less than a month after Apple stunned Wall Street with a $120 million loss in the first quarter of fiscal 1997.*
>
> *Amelio did not provide specifics about the restructuring or how many jobs might be cut as Apple seeks to cut costs. But he said the company planned to suspend the executive bonus plan until Apple returned to profitability. Recently, Apple said they expect to begin making a profit again by the end of the 1997 fiscal year in September. The decision to suspend the cash payout came shortly after Apple revealed some executives received substantial bonuses following a reported and an unexpected profit for the fourth quarter fiscal 1996. The payout was the result of a change in the compensation plan, which allowed the executives to receive bonuses based on the company's fourth quarter rather than full-year results.*
>
> *For the fourth quarter, which ended in September, Apple reported a profit of $25 million, surprising Wall Street, which had been expecting the company to report a modest loss.*

> *Much of the profits however came from a one-time gain Apple recognized for an inventory adjustment. Without that, Apple would have reported a modest loss or broken even, one analyst estimated.*
>
> *Based on that one profitable quarter, Apple's senior executives received "175 percent of their special bonus target," according to Apple's proxy statement. Amelio, who had a separate compensation agreement with the company, received a $648,000 bonus on top of his $990,000 base salary. Apple did not disclose the bonuses of the other executives. Apple officials said the special bonus plan was met to encourage executives to meet their turnaround goals.*

The announcement to curtail executive bonuses was explained by Wall Street as an attempt to head off a potential shareholder suit over the outrageous manipulation of earnings to justify a last-minute modified "executive bonus plan". The inventory adjustment that allowed Apple to report a "profit" was in accordance with generally accepted accounting principles (GAAP). In fact, the opportunity existed due to one of the basic rules of accounting product costing, although I am certain the Apple executives' intention did not match that of the GAAP in regard to fair and consistent reporting.

As an ex-auditor, former corporate controller, and accounting professor, I understand clearly how GAAP inventory rules invite earnings manipulation. Year-end games to maximize bonus potential are common practice, but Apple's executives crossed the line. It is time for responsible corporate boards to create executive bonus plans tied directly to real return on investment (ROI), not paper profits accomplished with accounting sleight of hand. The use of direct costing for internal inventory valuation would end much of the controversy; Chapter 8 demonstrates the ease of converting from absorption costing to direct costing or throughput accounting to report internal financial information.

In most cases, management decisions are made in earnest attempts to maximize short-run company performance, but, with the erroneous allocations reflected in product costing and profit reporting, these companies' poor decisions reflect the quality of the information used to make them. Every business operation is a series of events, a chain, which in concert produce a product. Each link cannot be looked at or measured in isolation but must be evaluated based on its relationship to the whole. This is the major principle of the Theory of Constraints and is just common sense. Financial accounting is not attempting to make an analysis of the chain of events and does not claim to be forward looking. The purpose of GAAP is to present a report of the past in a consistent and fair format. GAAP reporting records historical events and mathematically assigns a monetary value to the activity that has already taken place. *The theory behind financial accounting is valid for the purpose of reporting past activities; however, the actions necessary to maximize throughput and cash flow now and in the future are not the same as minimizing local unit cost and maximizing short-run reported net income.* If management is going to take local actions and make decisions that maximize future throughput rather than short-term reported net income, an entirely different measurement and feedback system must be designed and implemented. The new measurement and information system must accomplish what standard cost accounting measures and efficiency reporting does not:

> *The measurement and feedback system must be designed around maximizing throughput throughout the entire manufacturing operation, not unit-cost minimization. Product is not throughput until it is sold and shipped. Building inventory is not the goal; throughput is. Pushing inventory into the pipeline or supply chain without the market demand for the product is not the goal. Inventory valuation can be used to manipulate reported earnings, but the truth is always reflected in the cash flow.*

There are four basic concepts of financial cost accounting. Understanding the four basic concepts and how they distort or work against common-sense management decisions to optimize throughput is the key to diffusing their use for internal decision-making. This does *not* mean they should not be used for external reporting. These principles are the core of financial accounting product costing and are part of required reporting standards to ensure standardization and provide a consistent reference framework for comparison of historical performance. What it does mean is that they should *not* be used to reward or measure management or to make local operations or strategic decisions. Cost accounting was never intended to be used for internal decision-making, which is why the entire field of management accounting exists. Unfortunately, the entire field of management accounting has taken a back seat to financial accounting due to the power and prestige associated with the American Institute of Certified Public Accountants (AICPA). Universities have skewed their course offerings and emphasis toward producing Certified Public Accountants (CPAs) vs. Certified Management Accountants (CMAs), despite the fact that fewer than 15% of accounting graduates will work in public accounting. The core accounting curriculum at most major universities requires only one quarter of management accounting. Cost accounting usually takes up half of the management accounting course plus two full quarters of its own. Cost accounting is emphasized throughout the rest of the required accounting practice and theory courses. It is no wonder we don't know how to apply the concepts of management accounting in industry.

The four basic financial accounting concepts governing product costing are

1. Historical cost
2. The matching principle of revenues and expenses
3. Accrual accounting and revenue recognition
4. Cost allocation

The purpose of traditional financial accounting is to provide consistent and uniform information to stockholders, regulatory agencies, and lenders. As such, the information must reflect the historical cost of all of the resources consumed during the period being reported and must then be matched against the revenues generated during the same time frame. Historical cost and the matching principal are the reason why product cost allocation exists. The accounting of assets generated and consumed is reported through historical monetary values applied in a manner consistent with the matching principle.

Traditional accounting uses historical cost to record an asset at the time of purchase, and the expense (the consumption or use of the asset within the accounting period) is spread over numerous accounting periods based on the estimated life of the asset. The allocation choices used to depreciate the asset or assign it to a particular product produced are varied and, as they represent a fixed cost, are also arbitrary.

In other words, the sunk costs from previous strategic decisions are allocated over future periods to products as they are produced. Resource assets can be plant and equipment or people and all manufacturing support functions. Departments such as maintenance, tooling, production control, purchasing, quality control, storage and handling, and all plant supervision and engineering are resource assets that are allocated to the cost of the product rather than expensed in the period the work or utilization occurred. This entire bundle of cost allocation is known as manufacturing overhead and, in economic terms, is a fixed cost. This means the overhead cost does not vary as production volume increases or decreases, nor can day-to-day decisions and actions change the historical investment a company has in fixed costs. Overhead cost is a strategic, long-term investment to support the infrastructure of being in business.

Using TOC Logic To Determine Batch Sizes

Long-term strategic investments do not have a relationship to short-term volume, and no decisions on their use or evaluations on how well they were used can be understood from standard product costing. The use of cost accounting allocation to evaluate local area performance is probably the most misunderstood and misused concept in cost accounting.

Following is a case study of a company using a traditional "cost" orientation to determine production batch sizes. Other than overtime, the manufacturing overhead cost or cash outflow to maintain the infrastructure does not fluctuate in the following example, which is intended to show the very different outcome when decisions are based on throughput vs. minimizing unit cost. The plant and equipment investment base are the same in both scenarios — every person on the payroll got paid and the heat and lights were turned on every day. The

Table 4.1. Batch Case Sales Order Data

Product	Setup Time (hr)	Unit Run Time (min)	Order Base			
			Jan.	Feb.	March	April
A	10	5	300	100	400	500
B	5	5	250	50	60	400
C	20	10	250	250	250	250
D	2	2	150	100	50	50
E	10	10	50	50	50	50
Total			1000	550	810	1250

only difference is the choice in regard to capacity utilization and the effect on cash flow and reported net income.

The following company has five products with varying setup and run times. There currently are 4 months of firm orders. Only one resource has both a high capital investment and requires significant setup time. Sales order and product data are shown in Table 4.1.

Under our first scenario, the company has created a policy to minimize setup and unit cost. The policy batches product work orders in sizes designed to minimize time spent in setup to 15%. The policy ensures that each resource is producing product 85% of the time. Batch-size policies are common practice. The batch-size calculation is a function of the time needed to perform the setup. If product A uses 10 hours to set up, and the setup is 15% of the run time, then the batch should be sized to run approximately 57 hours, a ratio of 15% setup to 85% run time. If each unit requires 5 minutes of run time, then the batch size for 57 hours is approximately 680 units. The plant capacity is based on running one 8-hour shift, 5 days a week, for a 40-hour work week, or 160 hours a month. Table 4.2 details the production, throughput, and inventory for 4 months under the policy of minimum batch size. February's throughput includes January's late orders for products C, D, and E. The model assumes the orders were accepted late by the customer even though they were shipped late. In addition, the example assumes there is no constraint either before or after this operation. If such a bottleneck existed, the excess inventory would not end up as finished goods but as excess work in process. The result would be lower throughput units for February, March, and April.

Table 4.3 reflects production and shipments *without* a batching policy. Orders are scheduled based on due date and capacity availability. Figure 4.1 shows comparisons of cash flow and reported earnings between the batch and no-batch policies. Other basic assumptions include: (1) monthly fixed overhead including labor is $100,000, (2) the selling price is $200 per unit, and (3) raw material costs are $80 per unit.

Table 4.2. Batch Case Production, Sales, and Inventory Units Using a Minimum Batch Size Policy

		January				February			
Product	Batch Size	Units	Setup (hr)	Run (hr)	Total (hr)	Units	Setup (hr)	Run (hr)	Total (hr)
A	680	680	10	57	67	0	7	0	7
B	340	340	5	28	33	0	0	0	0
C	680	240	20	40	60	440	0	73	73
D	340	0	0	0	0	340	2	11	13
E	340	0	0	0	0	340	10	57	67
Total		**1260**	**35**	**125**	**160**	**1120**	**19**	**141**	**160**
Product shipped		790				760			
Inventory		470				830			
Unused capacity					0				0

		March				April			
Product	Batch Size	Units	Setup (hr)	Run (hr)	Total (hr)	Units	Setup (hr)	Run (hr)	Total (hr)
A	680	680	3	57	60	48	10	4	14
B	340	340	5	28	33	0	0	0	0
C	680	282	20	47	67	398	0	66	66
D	340	0	0	0	0	340	2	11	13
E	340	0	0	0	0	340	10	57	67
Total		**1302**	**28**	**132**	**160**	**1126**	**22**	**136**	**160**
Product shipped		810				1250			
Inventory		1322				1198			
Unused capacity					0				0

The difference in reported net income and the balance sheet values is due to the decision to build inventory. The overhead cost of operations assigned to inventory is the only reason for the difference in reported net income of $99,656 (Figure 4.1). The cash flow difference of $95,826 is solely from the increase in the dollar value of $95,826 invested in the raw materials in the ending inventory. The total of the cash flow and net income differences equals the total value in the ending inventory $195,482 ($99,656 + $95,826). This example understates the difference in cash flow and net income. *At the very least, some additional cost increase due to obsolescence, scrap, and storage and the increased cost of capital to finance the inventory would increase the difference in cash flow and income between the two scenarios.* The example ignores these costs, as they are impossible to quantify in a general example but could be relatively

Table 4.3. Batch Case Production, Sales, and Inventory Units Scheduled by Customer Due Date

Product	January Units	Setup (hr)	Run (hr)	Total (hr)	February Units	Setup (hr)	Run (hr)	Total (hr)
A	300	10	25	35	100	10	8	18
B	250	5	21	26	50	5	4	9
C	250	20	42	62	250	0[a]	42	42
D	150	2	5	10	100	2	3	5
E	50	10	8	26	50	10	8	18
Total	**1000**	**47**	**101**	**148**	**550**	**27**	**65**	**92**
Product shipped	1000				550			
Inventory	0				0			
Unused capacity				12				68

Product	March Units	Setup (hr)	Run (hr)	Total (hr)	April Units	Setup (hr)	Run (hr)	Total (hr)
A	400	0[a]	33	33	500	10	42	· 52
B	60	5	5	10	400	5	33	38
C	250	20	42	62	250	0[a]	42	42
D	50	2	2	4	50	2	2	4
E	50	10	8	18	50	10	8	18
Total	**810**	**37**	**90**	**127**	**1250**	**27**	**127**	**154**
Product shipped	810				1250			
Inventory	0				0			
Unused capacity				33				6

[a] The 0 setup time assumes the last product run the prior month becomes the first product run the next month and no setup is required.

high in industries where engineering changes are common and product life-cycles are short.

The example also ignores the possibility of a constraint after the high setup resource. If there is no bottleneck after the resource, the constraint is in the marketplace. The company can make more than the market will purchase, in which case increasing inventory serves no purpose other than to deplete cash. If a bottleneck exists after the high-setup resource, the throughput, reported earnings, and on-time delivery percentage would be lower for the batch scenario.

Based on the two scenarios, which plant has greater flexibility and would be better able to respond to the following list of "Murphy's" or opportunities?

Batching to Optimize Setup	Jan	Feb	Mar	April	Total 4 Mo's
Gross Sales	$ 158,000	$ 152,000	$ 162,000	$ 250,000	$ 722,000
Cost of Material	$ (63,200)	$ (60,800)	$ (64,800)	$ (100,000)	$ (288,800)
Overhead Cost	$ (65,726)	$ (63,230)	$ (67,390)	$ (103,997)	$ (300,344)
Profit/(Loss)	$ 29,074	$ 27,970	$ 29,810	$ 46,003	$ 132,856
Units Produced	1,260	1,120	1,302	1,126	4,808
Units Sold	790	760	810	1,250	3,610
Ending Inventory Units	470	830	1,322	1,198	1,198
Ending Inventory Dollars	$ 76,703	$ 135,441	$ 215,731	$ 195,482	$ 195,482
Cash Inflow/(Outflow) for Month	$ (47,629)	$ (30,768)	$ (50,480)	$ 66,252	
Cash Position at Month End	$ (47,629)	$ (78,398)	$ (128,878)	$ (62,626)	$ (62,626)
On Time Delivery	79%	100%	100%	100%	94%
Resource Efficiency Utilization	100%	100%	100%	100%	100%

No Batching Policy	Jan	Feb	Mar	April	Total 4 Mo's
Gross Sales	$ 200,000	$ 110,000	$ 162,000	$ 250,000	$ 722,000
Cost of Material	$ (80,000)	$ (44,000)	$ (64,800)	$ (100,000)	$ (288,800)
Overhead Cost	$ (100,000)	$ (100,000)	$ (100,000)	$ (100,000)	$ (400,000)
Profit/(Loss)	$ 20,000	$ (34,000)	$ (2,800)	$ 50,000	$ 33,200
Units Produced	1,000	550	810	1,250	3,610
Units Sold	1,000	550	810	1,250	3,610
Ending Inventory Units	-	-	-	-	-
Ending Inventory Dollars	$ -	$ -	$ -	$ -	$ -
Cash Inflow/(Outflow) for Month	$ 20,000	$ (34,000)	$ (2,800)	$ 50,000	
Cash Position at Month End	$ 20,000	$ (14,000)	$ (16,800)	$ 33,200	$ 33,200
On Time Delivery	100%	100%	100%	100%	100%
Resource Efficiency Utilization	92%	58%	79%	96%	81%

Summary of Results	With Batch Policy	With No Batch Policy		Difference
Gross Sales	$ 722,000	$ 722,000	$	-
Cost of Material	$ (288,800)	$ (288,800)		
Overhead Cost	$ (300,344)	$ (400,000)	$	99,656
Profit/(Loss)	$ 132,856	$ 33,200	$	99,656
Units Produced	4,808	3,610		1,198
Units Sold	3,610	3,610		-
Ending Inventory Units	1,198	-		1,198
Ending Inventory Dollars:				
Raw Material	$ 95,840	$ -	$	95,840
Overhead	$ 99,656	$ -	$	99,656
Total Ending Inventory	$ 195,496	$ -	$	195,496
Cash Position-Plus/(Negative)	$ (62,626)	$ 33,200	$	(95,826)
On Time Delivery	94%	100%		
Resource Efficiency Utilization	100%	81%		

Figure 4.1. Batch Case Comparative Financial Statement and Cash Flow Results

1. A customer changing its order
2. Engineering change in tooling or product feature
3. New product opportunity
4. Process improvement

5. Preventive maintenance
6. Cross-training or new employee training
7. Product obsolescence
8. Drop-in rush order

Which approach is more likely to use overtime to respond to any of the above situations? Which plant would feel more pressure to add capacity? Which scenario makes the most sense to you? Which scenario gives management the best visibility and opportunity to manage their operations, market, and cash flow?

The point of the example is to show how product cost allocation and decisions based on minimizing unit cost encourage excess inventory, distort reported net income vs. real cash flow, and reduce the ability of the manufacturing operation to respond to market opportunity and random disruption. If you add an internal constrained resource, the negative effects would be even more dramatic.

A New Unit Cost Measurement Using Old Management Accounting Concepts

What could we measure using management accounting with a TOC emphasis? First, we would have to identify the relevant information and then we would have to identify where the constraint is by asking:

1. What are the differences in cash flow in the future between the alternative actions?
2. Where is the constraint?

There are three relevant places for the constraint that can be applied to the example above:

1. An external constraint (in the example, the market is an external constraint, as there is more productive capacity than the market will buy)
2. An internal constraint before or after the high-setup resource (an option discussed above)
3. An internal constraint that *is* the high-setup resource (an option not previously discussed)

Under each of these possibilities, the following proposed measure would generate the appropriate unit cost as it relates to return on investment and cash flow and encourage the correct local actions:

$$\text{Throughput unit cost} = \text{period operating cash outflow/} \\ \text{period throughput units}$$

Table 4.4. Batch Case Throughput Unit Cost Over 4 Months

	No Batch	Batch	Difference
Throughput units (units shipped)	3610	3610	0
Cash for raw materials ($80/unit)	$288,800	$384,640	$95,840
Cash for fixed overhead	$400,000	$400,000	0
Throughput unit cost	$191	$217	$26

Throughput unit cost for the above example is shown in Table 4.4. If the constraint were after the high-setup resource, the number of throughput units could go down for both examples, but the cash flow difference would remain proportionally the same or might even improve for the no-batch scenario. The result could be a higher unit cost for each, but the proportionate difference would remain the same. Additionally, the lowest throughput unit cost would result from limiting the flow of product to the rate of the constraining resource, which would equal the new throughput rate. This would decrease the cash outflow for the raw materials cost by decreasing the excess work in process. *This unit cost cannot be used for making product profitability decisions!* It is does not consider the constrained capacity resources and is *not* a justification for allocating overhead to the product.

The purpose of throughput unit cost is to tie managers to their decisions to use cash to build inventory. There is no benefit for building inventory that is not needed now; in fact, there is a tremendous downside. Managers are not rewarded or encouraged to build inventory, and the temptation to manipulate net profit, in the short run, is eliminated.

If the market wanted more of the existing products or an additional new product was introduced and the constraining resource was the high-setup resource, we would make the most throughput by exploiting the high-setup resource. If the high-setup resource is the constraint, we should batch the product to increase run time and decrease setup time. This is the second step in TOC, known as *exploitation*.

Measuring throughput unit cost would correctly record the lowest unit cost under this scenario also. The measurement clearly uses the basics of management accounting, chooses the relevant information, and considers the limiting factor. The point to re-emphasize is that we cannot have measures that do not take into account the reality of our environment. TOC creates a framework for a company to examine its current operating environment and challenge the assumptions around how they are currently managing vs. how they could best manage their resources. Logically diagramming the conflict using the cloud technique easily reveals current management assumptions regarding their existing environment and how best to manage the resources.

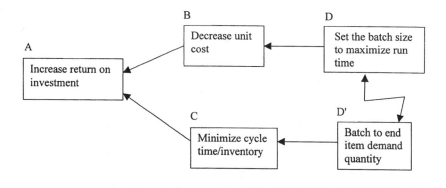

Figure 4.2. Batch Case Conflict Cloud

Figure 4.2 shows the cloud format for the above example. The cloud would read A to B to D as follows: To increase return on investment, I must decrease my unit cost. To decrease my unit cost, I must artificially set my batch sizes to maximize run time.

The A to C to D' side would be read as follows: To increase return on investment, I must decrease my cycle time/inventory. To decrease my cycle time/inventory, I must batch to the end-item demand quantity.

As the cloud in Figure 4.2 clearly demonstrates, the conflict is obvious: the company cannot batch to meet end-item demand and artificially set the batch size to minimize unit cost. But, it is the assumptions under the arrows that hold the key to the best solution. If the constraint is internal and is the high-setup resource, ROI will be maximized if batch size is determined to maximize run time on the constraint. If the constraint is in the marketplace or at a resource other than the high-setup resource, then batches based on end-item demand or batches that exploit the "real" internal constrained resource will maximize ROI. In any of the above scenarios, throughput unit cost conveys the best cost information to tie the batching decision to ROI.

There is no absolute wrong or right answer! The answer is dependent on the operating environment of the individual situation. To create the new measures that link local actions and decisions to ROI, companies must have the ability to consistently and continuously challenge their actions regarding their current environment. This is the power of the new TOC environment and the challenge a company must master to make TOC practical and sustainable. The companies that have done this are astoundingly successful. Chapters 6 and 7 explain a methodology that allows companies to use TOC to challenge work policies, practices, and measures throughout the organization.

Financial accounting has never claimed it is a forward-looking decision-making tool. Financial accounting is successful in attempting to assign monetary values to a specific period in a consistent and logical manner. As a gauge to measure real-time decisions, to reward local action, and to make strategic resource decisions, all the experts agree that financial accounting is a flop. So why do we keep on using the standard cost data we know are wrong? Because management does not have any other methodology to control costs!

Compare the unit cost results with the actual cash outlay for operations overhead for both of the scenarios for production. Minimizing unit cost did not help control costs. In fact, it raised the overall cost of operations by increasing investment in inventory and did not add to throughput. Also, the longer cycle time harmed throughput initially, and if internal bottlenecks existed then the total throughput, reported net income, and cash flow would have decreased. Labor overtime would have been necessary to attempt to meet on-time delivery goals in the first month and each successive month, given the internal bottleneck possibility.

Excess product, built to minimize unit cost, was stored as inventory and decreased cash flow substantially, but the reported financial results using standard product costing mask the actual financial health of the company. Is this a healthy organization that is meeting its commitments to its stakeholders? No! The excess product produced is valued at full standard cost, and a large portion of plant expenses for the month are reclassified as an inventory asset on the balance sheet. Reported income "looks" good! Assets "look" good!

In standard cost accounting, the overhead allocation is assigned to all products and becomes part of the cost of the product, along with the raw material cost. The product cost is removed from the expense category and redefined as an asset. Recognition of the expense of the production of the inventory takes place when the product is sold. This is known as *revenue recognition* and reinforces a basic principle of financial accounting known as *matching*. The expense of the inventory is matched to the time period of the sale of the product. Expenses are matched to the time frame of the revenue generation. This means the expense of building the product will not appear in the financial statements until the corresponding sale of the inventory is recorded. Cash outflow, in the time period the product is built, will not match the time period of the expense recognition in the income statement. In financial accounting, expense reporting and the actual timing of cash outflows have very little relationship to each other.

Reporting according to generally accepted accounting principles rewards the building of inventory until the time period the excess inventory is sold. Conversely, in the time period the inventory buildup is sold, the reported earnings will take a double hit for overhead expense. The cost of goods sold will have the full $100,000 for the current month, plus $83 of allocated overhead for every unit sold that was produced in a previous period. The difference in reported net income is simply a timing difference as to when the overhead is recognized as an expense, but it is a powerful incentive for behavior. Many company's have attempted to hide declining sales and profits by building inventory, an action with a potential "time bomb" waiting in the "assets" category of the balance sheet.

The concept in financial accounting of *revenue recognition* means revenues are recognized when goods are exchanged (not when cash is received). The matching and recognition principles together result in another key concept known as *accrual accounting*. Accrual accounting defines profit as the difference between revenues and expenses, not cash receipts and cash payments. The need to match all product cost to product revenues in the time period the product is sold results in the concept of *cost* allocation. Because many different products share common resources, complex product-costing formulas have evolved. Matching expenses to revenues is the cause of a great deal of complexity in accounting systems and is the major cause of distortions in attempts to understand product cost. Simply stated, in the quest to better "cost" a product we have spent tremendous effort to add complexity without creating any value. In fact, we have created tremendous dysfunction and misinformation.

Universally, a time lag exists in all organizations between cash and accrual accounting. Overhead expenses such as factory space, equipment, labor, and energy are allocated by formulas to facilitate the matching of operations expenses to the product produced in the accounting period. These product costs are then used to generate the cost-of-sales figures reported on the income statement when the product is sold. *The reality is that the actual matching of expenses is unknown and unknowable.* For example, it is impossible to know how much of the computing expenses were spent on purchasing material vs. personnel information requirements vs. scheduling product vs. updating engineering bills of material to support which, if any, individual product. More importantly, the computing hardware, software, and staff exist as part of the strategic investment decision to support production of any and all products. The investment was not a short-term decision but a long-term strategic decision, and the cost of last month's computing is a sunk cost, unrecoverable and gone. Cross-charging departments for the fully allocated use of internal assets can cause the user department to make decisions that negatively impact cash flow, return on investment, and even competitive advantage.

The method of cost allocation often determines the use or lack of use of a resource and can determine response prioritization from departments supporting production (maintenance, tooling, engineering, information systems). Chapter 1 references an example of how high cost allocation caused a strategic resource to be underutilized and outside resources to be purchased because the cost allocated internally was greater than the cash outflow to the external vendor. In essence, the company had paid for the service twice and perhaps subsidized a competitor. This was not the intended result when the strategic tactics were planned and the investment decision was made.

A standard practice in companies is to focus maintenance, tooling, cross-training priorities, setup reduction programs, and quality improvement processes at the resource or department with the highest standard overhead cost rate or the highest dollar investment. Improvement at the high-dollar-investment work center can dramatically improve the reported cost per unit of product produced at the work station but will not improve throughput or increase cash flow if the process was not the constraining resource. In fact, you may end up spending more cash to invest in more inventory to protect your new efficiency rating. There will be no return on the investment, because there was no gain in shippable product. To receive recognition for the unit part cost reduction from the improvement, the resource must be kept running at its maximum rate. If this resource is not the constraint, downstream processes will be flooded with excess work in process. This is backwards from maximizing ROI and violates common sense, yet it is common practice.

Overhead Cost Allocation in Product Costing

The different potential variations of product costing systems are beyond the scope of this book. I would have to write at least three chapters covering material that is already in every cost accounting text on the market and would add nothing to this experience. Instead, I am going to take a very simplistic view. A solid, basic understanding of product cost allocation is critical to tackle this universal conflict common to every managed organization.

Product costing hybrids abound in industry, and I believe I have seen every variation there is. All product cost allocation is some basic variation of the following criteria, regardless of which of the following the company uses:

1. A standard costing system computes direct labor, raw materials, and overhead at a standard rate for inventory and product cost valuation.
2. A normal costing system computes overhead at a standard rate, but raw materials and direct labor are at actual cost for inventory and product cost valuation.
3. An actual costing system uses no standard rates. The example at the beginning of the chapter is an example of using actual cost to value inventory and product cost.

The smallest cost collection unit is the cost center. Cost centers are classified as either production or service. Production cost centers, by definition, actually add a unit of work to the product such as assembly or welding, and a service department supports the production departments with such activities as maintenance, tooling, inventory control, or material storage and handling. All costs go through a first-tier allocation and are identified according to their origination in an individual cost center. This means they are specifically assigned to the cost center that caused them to happen. Shared resource costs, such as building maintenance, insurance, heat, and lights, are allocated to each cost center on a

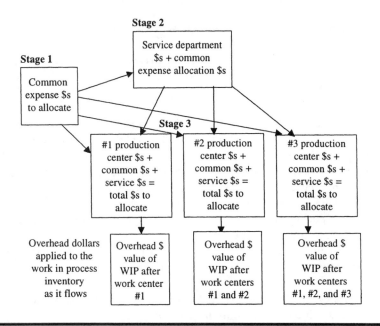

Figure 4.3. Cost-Accounting Overhead Allocation Flow Diagram

pro rata basis using a common denominator such as square footage taken up by a department or the number of employees, etc. The result of the first-tier allocation is that all shared expenses are assigned to either a production or service cost center.

The second stage is to allocate service department cost centers to production cost centers. The service departments' costs are allocated to the producing departments according to an allocation base that can be as simple as direct labor hours or as complicated as an activity-based costing concept such as using the number of individual transactions from material storage or the number of engineering work orders. Simple or complex, the bulk of the expenses in the cost center do not have any direct relationship to the allocation base. They are arbitrarily allocated. After the second stage, all manufacturing support costs are assigned to production cost centers, and total costs are ready to be allocated to each unit of product based on either an actual or a budgeted standard of time each product spends in the production cost center. Figure 4.3 shows a general flow of overhead allocation.

Standard product costing results in three possible variances to analyze:

1.   The *production volume variance* reflects how well actual production followed planned production. Did we produce as many units as we planned?

2. The *spending variance* shows how accurate the fixed costs budget is. Did we spend more on fixed overhead than we budgeted?
3. The *usage variance* reflects actual performance to standard for the production department. On average, did we use more than the budgeted inputs of material, labor, or machine time to produce each part?

The variance does not explain why the variance occurred, what caused it, or even if it is "good" or "bad" for the overall goal of the company. As explained in the purchase price variance example in Chapter 1, variances are often interconnected and can have inverse relationships. The quality of materials can have a direct effect on the favorable or unfavorable variance generated in operation labor and machine usage. An unfavorable purchase price variance for exceptional quality material can result in favorable variances for labor and machine usage and vice versa.

Cost accounting breaks product costs down into three categories for allocation purposes:

1. Raw materials (material that is used in the production of the product and is incorporated into the finished good product)
2. Direct labor (labor cost added when the product passes through a production cost center)
3. Overhead (allocated per the three-stage allocation described above)

Product raw material cost is assigned to the product based on a standard number of feet, pounds, etc. required to build the product at a standard cost per pound or foot. The actual feet or pounds used, compared against the standard feet or pounds, is known as a usage variance. If more than standard is used, the variance is unfavorable. If less than standard is used, the variance is favorable. If the actual price paid per foot or pound is less or more than the standard, the price variance is favorable or unfavorable. The usage variance is used to gauge the performance of the producing department, and the price variance is used to gauge the performance of the purchasing department.

Purchasing is measured on their ability to produce favorable raw materials price variances. To minimize cost, purchasing has several options, such as purchasing in large lots to obtain quantity discounts or shopping around for the low-cost vendor. Factors such as on-time delivery, obsolescence, storage and handling costs, quality, short lead times, and process suitability are secondary, if they are considered at all, which finally happens when the purchasing process becomes so out of whack that a "new program" or "key indicator" is implemented to correct the situation. All of the above factors are real components of the true cost of raw materials and can dramatically effect throughput and ROI.

Direct labor cost is assigned to the product based on a standard number of hours required to produce the product. The usage variance for direct labor is computed in the exact same manner as the raw materials variance. The actual hours used are compared against the standard hours budgeted. The actual price per hour of labor is compared against the standard labor rate. "Favorable" means you spent or used less than the standard and "unfavorable" means more was spent or used than planned. Both the usage and the price variances are used to gauge the performance of the producing department.

These variances can create excess cost and incorrectly reward or punish. If purchasing is rewarded for creating favorable purchase price variances, then there are two predictable outcomes or effects from the behavior that purchasing will exhibit to pursue maximizing favorable purchase price variances. The first behavior is large volume buys in order to receive volume discounts on pricing. The second is that, in order to purchase the least cost raw material, sacrifices in supplier reliability or quality of material might be made. Both of these behaviors and their undesirable effects have been clearly researched and documented as the "hidden costs of inventory". The view that inventory is evil has fueled the drive to lower inventory levels at all cost. Neither of these behaviors helps control cost; they simply increase waste and decrease ROI.

Machine utilization is assigned to the product based on a standard number of hours required to produce the product. The usage variance is computed in exactly the same manner as labor and raw materials. The actual time used is compared against the standard for the usage variance. The usage variance is used to gauge the efficient use of automated areas that are machine intensive. Machine-intensive areas usually have high fixed overhead costs, reinforcing the belief that maximizing the use of the machinery (running it all of the time) will result in the organization being the low-cost producer, thus leading to a competitive advantage in the market place. The least-cost assumption is flawed if the concept is applied to any area other than the constrained resource or if the constraint is in the marketplace and not in the plant. This is clearly demonstrated by the example of batching to minimize unit cost found at the beginning of this chapter.

Another example of the difference in focus provided by the least-cost mindset vs. TOC is the practice of prioritizing improvement efforts to reduce time per part at high dollar investment resources. If the machine resource is not the constrained resource, setup reduction efforts are generally wasted, and improvement programs seldom show bottom-line results. The Total Quality Management (TQM) team will be focused on these high dollar visibility areas because of the large impact on reducing local unit costing. The excellent problem-solving tools of TQM are rendered ineffective, and considerable effort and valuable resources are wasted because the improvement does not significantly contribute to the company's ability to increase throughput. Misdirected focus, not misguided process techniques, should be blamed for the majority of TQM failures in relationship to generating bottom-line results.

Product cost allocations, variance reporting, and local efficiency measures result in a distorted picture for organizational decision-making and inaccurately assess the effectiveness of management's strategic and local operation decisions. At the end of any year, a company's historical performance will be the same no matter what method of cost allocation they use, but the decisions made from that information will obviously affect future results. The results of any company's performance are the sum total of the decisions and local actions at each department level. Each department or local operator's action is a reflection of their measure or perceived measure. Whatever measures the company is reporting, posting, or gathering will influence the actions people take to maximize their performance measures. If there are no measures, people will still try to maximize the efficiency of their process because they make the basic assumption that maximizing their area performance will best maximize ROI for the entire company.

The concept of maximizing output per machine hour and labor hour or local resource efficiency is deeply ingrained in the American manufacturing mentality. The labor force becomes very uncomfortable if they are experiencing idle time. The logical conclusion made by the labor force is that a layoff is around the corner. Management is very uncomfortable if people or machinery are idle. Their conclusion is that capacity is being wasted and the costs are going up. Both labor and management are solidly entrenched in the belief that every resource must be operating at full productive capacity or the company is not exploiting its ability to generate a return on its investment. This is known as local optima (see Figure 4.4). Local variance analysis and efficiency measures only serve to institute, reinforce, and support local optima behavior. Ultimately, there has been no other option for management to tie local actions to maximizing the performance of the organization until the ability to apply the practicality of TOC was developed.

Maintenance, tooling, and quality have prioritized their efforts, either on the belief that everything has the same priority (first in, first out) or the most expensive operation should be top priority. Obviously, under a measure that emphasizes least cost, the most expensive and overhead-intensive areas will receive priority. This is not a common-sense method of prioritizing, because it ignores basic systems theory, the laws of physics, and the leverage points of the business. The area with the greatest ability to impact overall plant throughput (the constraint) is the most effective area on which to focus improvement processes and the only place to maximize efficient resource utilization.

The use of local efficiency and standard cost-variance analysis is the cause of the majority of chronic conflicts outlined in Chapter 2 and detailed in the spider web conflict cloud (Figure 2.2). Re-examining the conflicts in the spider web clouds exposes their relationship to standard and unit-cost accounting practices. The central reason for the widespread use of standard cost reporting is the need for management to minimize and control cost. This chapter should convince you that minimizing local unit cost does not lead to controlling costs. In fact, the exact opposite happened in each of the examples presented in this chapter. Cash flow can significantly decrease due to focusing plant operations

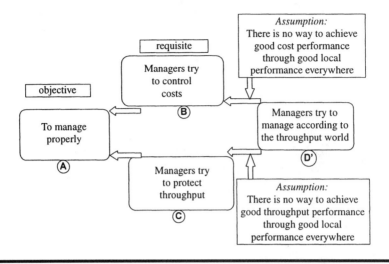

Figure 4.4. Resolution of the Local vs. Global Optima Cloud (©Eli Goldratt)

on minimizing unit cost. On-time delivery and throughput are negatively impacted, and the probability of overtime expenditures increases.

The unit-cost conflict has resulted in operations managers attempting to find a compromise between trying to ship on time by expediting orders through the plant and trying to minimize unit cost by running maximum loads on all resources. Any seasoned operations manager will concede that this is the case, and it ultimately results in wasted effort and dollars. The problem is that they do not see that they have viable options to solve the conflicts and they find themselves fighting fires daily.

Maximizing resource loads increases inventories and cycle time, which increases expediting and labor costs, all of which add up to decreasing cash flow and return on investment. If the minimum unit cost and local efficiency measures and practices are replaced with throughput measures and practices, there is no conflict for the production manager. Costs, as recognized by real cash flow, are controlled!

If managing according to the throughput world (managing the system as a dependent chain of events) both protects maximizing throughput and controlling cost, then we must replace the existing measures and reporting with measures and reporting that recognize the real and critical factors that govern throughput and ultimately the bottom line. If we do not do so, we will continue to have chronic conflict between the actions people need to take to do a good job and those actions necessary to maximize their measurements and thus be rewarded.

5 Drum-Buffer-Rope Basics and Predictable Implementation Effects

There is general consensus in industry on the need for change in measures and management accounting practice. The previous chapters clearly demonstrate that the common practice of using standard cost and efficiencies as the gauges to measure real-time decisions, reward local action, and make strategic resource decisions is less than optimal. I believe the reason companies continue to use the standard cost data, when they know the data are suboptimal, is because management does not have any other methodology to control costs and focus improvement efforts and investment decisions. There has been no other practical alternative to correlate local actions to maximizing the performance of the organization until the ability to apply the Theory of Constraints was developed.

The basic theory in throughput accounting and Drum-Buffer-Rope (DBR) scheduling mirrors the direct costing and incremental or relevant costing taught in any beginning management accounting course. The philosophy of exploiting the drum is based on the same principle expressed in every management accounting text regarding profit maximization when a limiting factor or scarce resource exists. Drum-Buffer-Rope is the practical application of the basic profit maximization principle of management accounting. This chapter offers a basic overview of the philosophy, terminology, and application of TOC manufacturing scheduling and the management tool, DBR.

The first step in any TOC solution is to find the constraint. The slowest resource in the production operation is the constrained capacity resource (the drum) and beats the cadence for the pace of the entire operation. Any operation outproducing the constraining resource only adds to expenses without contributing to the throughput of the organization. Individually maximizing all resource outputs results in large work-in-process inventories; long cycle times; increased labor, storage, and handling expenses; and a large investment in work-in-process inventory; it also requires a larger investment in raw materials inventory. The common thread in Just-in-Time (JIT), Total Quality Management (TQM), and TOC is that reducing inventories should be given priority over reducing operating expenses. Reducing inventories, other than strategic inventory necessary for protecting the release of material to the floor on time and to buffer the constraints, will decrease assets, increase throughput, and decrease operating expenses, all of which increase the return on investment to the organization.

Drum-Buffer-Rope ties a rope between the front-end resource and the slowest resource in the production line. The first resource can never outpace or overproduce the slower resource more than the length of the rope. Because all other resources are faster, they can sprint and close any gaps that might appear along the production line. This solution constrains all of the resources in front of the slowest to produce no faster, on average, than the slowest resource. More importantly, the rope prevents the work-in-process inventory in front of the slow resource from growing beyond the slack allowed in the length of the rope. By leaving slack in the rope, a protective buffer will open up just in front of the slowest resource. This concept is emphasized in both the movie and the book *The Goal* in the infamous Boy Scout hike with Herbie. Translating the scout troop analogy to the shop floor is not difficult. The problem is to provide excellent due-date performance while at the same time minimize inventories. If demand exceeds capacity, there must be at least one bottleneck. If an organization has excess work-in-process inventories or finished goods, then it must have excess capacity even if there are many late orders.

The planned buffer and buffer management are the key differences between JIT and DBR. The major drawback to JIT or assembly-line operations is that any workstation disruption will cause the entire line to stop. The buffers allowed in front of each workstation are very small, so when a disruption hits one workstation, all workstations will quickly exhaust their protective buffers and the entire line will grind to a halt. Simple variation in processing times creates problems. "Murphy" is the number one enemy of JIT. For this reason, an essential part of any conversion to JIT must include a systematic way to squeeze variation out of each and every individual workstation. The overall sources of disruption and fluctuation must be dealt with or the overall throughput can actually be less than before JIT. This is the reason for the emphasis on statistical process control, routine maintenance, fully cross-trained work forces, and other such factors in JIT systems. The implementation of all of these issues, including the necessary training, is the reason for the long lead times and large expenditures required to fully implement a functional JIT operation.

The Buffer Objective

The TOC solution for production management and scheduling begins with the basic premise that different resources have different capacities and that statistical fluctuations and disruption cannot realistically be eliminated. Any viable solution must be able to cope with these facts of production life. DBR is designed to protect the constrained capacity resource (CCR), the most overloaded resource. The difference between the definition of a bottleneck and the CCR can best be explained by the analogy of the height of the players on a professional basketball team. Although all are taller than the average human, there is still only one tallest person on the team. Even if all of the operations resources are booked over capacity, there is still one resource that is the most constrained — the CCR.

The CCR needs to be protected against two types of "Murphy": random disruption and non-instant availability of a resource. Non-instant availability means a resource is idle because it must wait for other resources to finish before it can begin. This can happen because resources are busy working on other orders or are waiting for outside vendor parts, raw materials, tooling, or setup changes. Minimizing these disruptions is accomplished by the strategic placement of three different buffers:

1. A buffer in front of the CCR
2. A buffer of non-CCR parts in front of assembly, if a CCR part is required in the assembly
3. A buffer of finished goods in front of shipping

The objective of the first buffer is to ensure that the CCR is not starved when "Murphy" strikes upstream. The objective of the second buffer is to ensure that all non-constrained capacity resource parts arrive and are waiting in front of assembly when the CCR part arrives. CCR parts should never be made early or be required to wait for a non-CCR part. The objective of the third buffer is to ensure on-time delivery in the event of disruption upstream of shipping.

Expediting According to the Buffer

To size the buffer properly, the arrival of parts to the buffer should be monitored and compared against the scheduled arrival time. Monitoring the buffer sends a signal to the plant as to when to expedite. When a job does not enter the buffer on schedule, it creates a "hole" in the buffer. Dividing the buffer into three zones is a critical aspect of buffer management. The first zone can be called the green zone; the second, the yellow zone; and the third, the red zone or the danger zone. Parts that do not arrive in the red zone on time are in danger of not being worked on by the CCR when scheduled and may end up shipping late. Holes in the green zone are *not* cause for concern. Holes in the yellow zone indicate an immediate need to locate the missing job and decide whether or not the job needs to be expedited. If the job will not arrive in the red zone of the buffer before it is scheduled at the CCR, then the job needs to be expedited. Management of the buffer focuses attention on late arrivals and indicates a clear path of action. A plan can be made to expedite if the job will not arrive in the buffer red zone on schedule. *Only* red zone holes are expedited.

Sizing the Buffer

Sizing the buffer has two risks. Undersizing the buffer leaves the CCR open to starvation and lost throughput for the entire plant. Oversizing the buffer increases operating expenses and cycle time and decreases inventory turns, resulting in decreased cash flow. Obviously, the first type of risk is the most expensive and the most damaging. In implementing DBR, it is better to err on the side of a conservative buffer. Proper sizing will occur by monitoring the buffer. During the initial estimation of part run-cycle times, being at least realistic and at best slightly inflated is preferred.

If all jobs are consistently arriving in the green and yellow zone, the buffer is too big and can safely be reduced. If jobs are consistently arriving late and in the red zone, the buffer needs to be increased. If all jobs are arriving late or in the red zone and the cause is consistently another operation, there is a strong possibility that the CCR has been identified erroneously and the cause of the disruption may be the actual CCR. Buffer management and monitoring will not allow the real CCR to hide.

System Improvements Through Buffer Management

Buffer management also allows the disruption in upstream processes to be quantified and systematically identified. Focusing improvements on the consistent causes of holes in the buffer, prioritized by first red then yellow, gives priority to maintenance, tooling, and setup time reduction and cross-training programs. This ongoing focus for process improvement allows a safe and continuous shrinking of cycle time and buffer size. Tracking holes in the buffer highlights problematic upstream resources and allows us to focus improvements at the resource. As the process is improved, holes in the buffer will disappear and allow the buffer size to be safely reduced, consistently decreasing cycle time and work in process. This is a continuous process improvement that results in increasing return on investment.

Protective Capacity of Non-Constrained Capacity Resources

The prioritizing of problematic resources, identified by buffer management, arranges resources in order of their lack of protective capacity. Protective capacity, also known as sprint capacity, is the excess amount of capacity all resources have in relationship to the CCR. By tracking holes in the buffer, we can get a fairly accurate picture of protective capacity throughout the plant without expensive time studies. This is important for several reasons:

1. The resource with the least protective capacity is where the bottleneck is most likely to move if the current CCR is permanently elevated.
2. Monitoring protective capacity of problematic resources will help determine how many setups are "free" or how small we can size the batches at non-CCRs, before we are in danger of creating a floating bottleneck (a bottleneck resource that mimics the CCR because of our mismanagement of the bottleneck resource).
3. It provides the ability to focus and prioritize improvement processes at non-CCR operations.
4. It provides a method for prioritizing the subordination process of bottleneck resources after the constrained capacity resource has been catered to.
5. It provides a method of estimating how much non-CCR protective capacity can be sold in a targeted market of non-CCR jobs. This is especially important if the company intends to identify excess capacity and target market non-CCR product to increase cash flow. This market can only be exploited to the extent that it does not erode the protective capacity and jeopardize on-time buffer performance in front of the CCR. Overselling a non-CCR product creates a floating bottleneck and jeopardizes the buffer in front of the CCR and ultimately throughput.

The Drum

Inherent in the Theory of Constraints is the implicit understanding that every and any system can only produce as quickly as its slowest resource. The production plant output is limited to the pace of the CCR. Just as there is only one tallest person on the basketball team, there is only one CCR. Eli Goldratt referred to the CCR as the drum because the CCR sets the pace or beats the cadence for the rest of the resource operations to follow.

This would be a good time to review the five-step process that is the governing framework for TOC and DBR, as the steps will be referred to continuously as the drum is explained:

1. Identify the systems constraint(s).
2. Exploit the constraint (maximize use of the constraint).
3. Subordinate all other processes to the decision to exploit the constraint.
4. Elevate the constraint.
5. Start all over at step one; do not let inertia become the constraint.

There are two criteria for a good production schedule:

1. The schedule must be realistic.
2. The schedule should be immune to a reasonable amount of disruption.

Applying TOC to the criteria of being realistic forces us to start with the first step and identify the system scheduling constraints. A client's due date for an order is the first constraint. The schedule must, by definition of the five-step process, subordinate all resources to our decision to commit a delivery date to our customers. Maximizing due-date performance and exploiting the CCR is the objective of the schedule. To accomplish step three, the decision to subordinate our manufacturing process to our decision to exploit shipping according to the customer due date requires returning to the first step in TOC — identify the constraint in the production process, the CCR, the drum. This is how DBR was designed using the five-step process of the TOC.

Once the drum is identified and the pace of all resources is subordinated to the pace of the drum, a realistic due date can be given to the customer. The estimated ship date is based on the next available time on the CCR, plus the time the order will take to move through the processes after the CCR. There is no possibility of shipping earlier unless a previously scheduled CCR job is bumped. Expediting simply shuffles who will be late. The entire system is constrained by the CCR, and promising due dates that exceed the available capacity of the CCR will result in due dates that are not met.

The Rope

The rope is the timed release of raw materials to the first operation to ensure the job will reach the buffer before the drum is scheduled to work on it. The rope can be thought of as chain of time and is diagrammed in Figure 5.1. The rope ties the first resource to the pace of the constraint, and the length of the

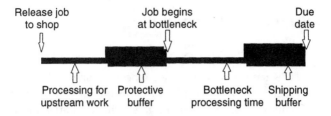

Figure 5.1. DBR Scheduling Flow Diagram

rope is the time required to keep the buffer full, plus the upstream processing time. For example, if the CCR buffer is sized to 8 hours and the upstream processes take 4 hours, then the materials must be released 12 hours before the job is due to begin processing at the CCR. The length of the rope is 12 hours and the slack in the rope, the buffer, is 8 hours.

The predictable and proven effects of implementing DBR include:

1. All machine and labor efficiencies at non-constraints will go down.
2. Work-in-process inventories will shrink.
3. Lead and cycle times will shrink.
4. Scheduling becomes easier.
5. Finished goods inventory can be reduced.
6. Batch sizes can be cut.
7. Cash flow will spiral up.
8. There is a one-time negative net income hit as the excess work-in-process and finished goods inventories are reduced and overhead stored in inventory is expensed through cost of goods sold.
9. Conflict with old measurements is immediate.
10. Excess capacity is exposed.
11. The process of ongoing improvement must be refocused to marketing and sales strategy as the constraint moves to the marketplace.
12. The competitive advantages of short cycle/lead times, on-time delivery, quality, and quick response to the market that are gained through DBR can be used to market the excess production capacity.

Drum-Buffer-Rope is not just a production solution but also offers the potential for a market solution! It is not sustainable unless the measurements and incentive systems throughout the company are changed to reflect a TOC management philosophy. Chapter 6 and 7 focus on how to align measures with these predictable effects and identify conflicts in the old measurement system in regard to the concepts of exploiting the constraint and subordinating actions of non-constraint resources to supporting the exploitation of the constraint.

Drum-Buffer-Rope Scheduling

Finding the Production CCR

Finding the CCR requires establishing a schedule horizon that approximates the current order cycle. If, on average, it takes one month from the time an order is taken until it is shipped, then a good schedule horizon is one month. The schedule horizon needs to include all orders due in the month, plus all orders started and in process up until the end of the month. This ensures that all jobs in process during the month are accounted for, including orders with ship dates beyond our one-month horizon that must begin process during the month in order to ship on time.

It is important that every resource operation only account for one setup per part number or operation, *not* per number of orders, when identifying the CCR. Initially, the objective is to identify the resource operation with the longest actual production cycle time, independent of the number of setups. When DBR is up and running, setups and batch sizes are functions of the schedule and will be determined as part of the ongoing dynamic process. One of the rules of DBR is that there will be no fixed setups or batch sizes at non-CCRs. The illustration in Chapter 4 using TOC logic to determine batch size clearly explains the criteria and the need for flexible decision-making regarding setups and batch sizes.

The load for each type of resource and resource availability during the time horizon are then calculated. If the load placed on any resource is greater that the resource availability, at least one bottleneck has been identified. The operation with the most overload is the capacity constrained resource.

Check the Data

The next step is to check the validity of the resource load against intuition. Both engineering and the shop foreman should review the data, but it is neither feasible nor necessary to ensure the accuracy of *all* the data. The CCR and any other identified bottlenecks, starting from the most overloaded to the least, can be used to prioritize the need for accurate information. The following items should be checked with regard to the resource load accuracy:

1. The accuracy of the number of resource units
2. Process time of the resource units (capacity)

Produce a report detailing what orders consume what percentage of the CCR (suspected, but not yet verified), and check the validity of the process times of the required parts and the accuracy of the sales order data used to drive the resource load report. It is important to verify the accuracy of the required time to produce the part at the resources with the people doing the task, *not* those who designed the task.

Once the suspected CCR has been identified, the job orders using the resource can be allocated based on the first due date for all orders. This is the same as calculating the load on the CCR only. The capability of exploding down from the sales order, by due date, to a resource is common in most Manufacturing Resource Planning (MRP) systems. Review Figure 5.2 for a picture of the jobs allocated to the CCR. The CCR load highlights the following:

1. Job orders in due date sequence
2. When and what jobs overload the CCR
3. How much the CCR is over capacity by specific date
4. Days that have excess CCR capacity capability

Remember that the CCR use cannot extend further into the future; otherwise, our constraint of shipping on time is violated. The next step is to shift all of the job orders backwards in time by priority of order due date. Review Figure 5.3 for a picture of the job allocation after the shift backwards. If some of the job orders have slid past the present date, start at the far left and shift all jobs to the right, filling in the empty spaces identifying available CCR capacity. This accomplishes two objectives:

1. The CCR scheduled peaks are shifted backwards until job orders are scheduled when capacity realistically exists.
2. All job orders were shifted forward to take advantage of unscheduled capacity.

Finally, a realistic CCR schedule exists that maintains due-date performance. A direct connection between the CCR and the current marketplace job orders has been established. Most importantly, the CCR schedule can be used to schedule the entire plant, and the schedule can be maintained and updated by tracking only the information necessary to schedule the CCR. The planned release date for job orders is determined by adding, to the date the order is scheduled to be processed at the CCR, the time needed to maintain the buffer, plus the cycle time of upstream non-CCR operations. Refer to the above section on sizing and managing the buffer for the guidelines on management and proper sizing of the buffers. Remember the safety net that monitoring the buffer provides in regard to the drum. If the wrong CCR has been identified, buffer management will quickly point out a resource with less capacity if jobs are consistently creating holes in the red zone.

Allocation of Raw Material Resource Stocks

Raw materials inventory availability is critical. The allocation of raw materials resource stocks needs to be based on the same first-come, first-served basis

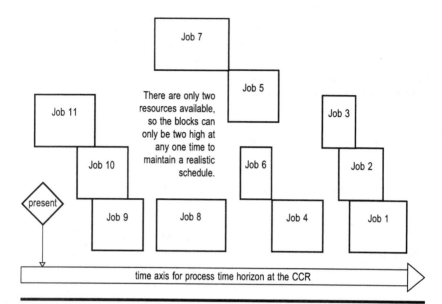

Figure 5.2. Jobs Assigned to the Constrained Capacity Resource by Customer Order Date

used to schedule jobs at the CCR. This clearly follows steps two (exploitation) and three (subordination of non-CCRs) to the needs of the drum. The CCR must rigidly follow the sequence derived from the schedule of job order priority. All other areas are dynamic to ensure that they take appropriate action to subordinate to our decision to exploit the drum (see Chapters 6 and 7 on exploitation and subordination, respectively). Remember, in comparison to the CCR, all other resources have excess capacity.

Case Study on Cutting Batch Sizes

When implementing constraints management scheduling, a misconception repeatedly surfaces in regard to batch sizes, and the constraint is often misidentified. During implementation of DBR in the weaving company (see Chapter 1), the team was split on their belief of where the constraint really resided. Weaving was convinced it was the looms, and the rest of the plant was convinced it was the small slitter. The process flow was as follows:

1. The looms wove the wire into 45-inch wide wire mesh in 500-foot rolls.
2. The clean line cleaned the cloth.
3. The large slitter slit the cloth into nine rolls, 5 inches wide.
4. The small slitter slit the 5-inch rolls into five rolls, 1 inch wide.

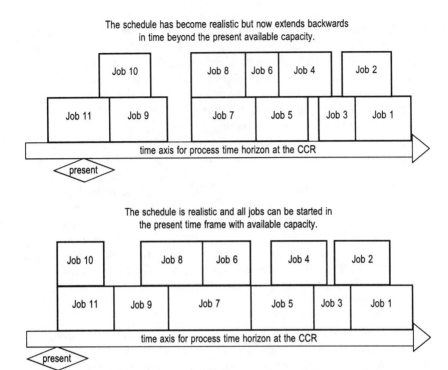

The schedule has become realistic but now extends backwards in time beyond the present available capacity.

The schedule is realistic and all jobs can be started in the present time frame with available capacity.

Figure 5.3. Jobs Scheduled on the Constrained Capacity Resource To Reflect Realistic Capacity Available

5. The 1-inch rolls can be sent to the automated area for final product assembly.
6. Or, the 1-inch rolls can be sent to shearing and cut into varying lengths to be sold as kits.
7. The final assembly product has five different mesh types requiring assembly.
8. The cut pieces have the same five different mesh types, slit into varying widths and then sheared into varying lengths.
9. There are two small slitters that can slit cloth for either the assembly area or the shearing area.

The two operations following the small slitter were routinely flooded and starved. This led the supervisor of slitting and the operations downstream to believe the small slitters in slitting were the constraint. The first clue that the small slitters bottleneck was a policy constraint and not a physical constraint was the alternate flooding and starving, not just starving. A policy constraint is a practice or policy regarding how to manage a resource, not the actual physical capacity of the resource. Either slit rolls arrived very early or very late at both workstations. Logically, if material is arriving early and late, the time spent running product early could have been spent producing product due now. If something arrives early, there is either excess capacity at the process delivering the product early or it is running the wrong priority product.

There were two policies constraining slitting:

1. Large batch sizes were run to minimize setups. If five different material types must be slit to feed downstream processes and any single missing item stops assembly, then halving the batch size allows the slitters to fill the buffer in the downstream process in half of the cycle time.
2. Deciding to break slitting into two areas and dedicate the large slitters to running the initial breakdown of material only was another decision to save on setups. Changeover at the large slitters took twice as long as the small slitters, and the company did not have the extra knives for the large slitters to set them to make the additional cuts required for small-width slits.

After breaking the policy constraints in slitting, starvation downstream was eliminated and the plant was able to focus on the looms. Again, the constraint turned out to be several policies. Both the looms and slitting required very small fixed-cost investments, such as extra knives for the slitters to allow the dedicated slitters to be set up to make small cuts as well as initial breakdowns of the rolls. Extra creels were purchased for the looms, allowing the setup time for looms to be reduced from 36 hours to 6. The extra creels allowed the wire spools to be preloaded on the additional creels. When a loom ran out of wire, the old creel could be removed and the new preset creel rolled into place; the only setup time required was wiring the loom. These changes resulted in the constraint moving to the finished-goods assembly machinery. The focus was moved to the assembly area, the true bottleneck, and led to the following focused improvements:

1. Breaking the policy constraint regarding batch sizes and offloading small cuts to the large slitters at the slitter operation allowed a buffer to be maintained in front of the assembly and ended starvation at the constraint.
2. Operators were trained on quickness of response to machine downtime in assembly and how to fix jams, which increased uptime at the constraint.
3. The assembly machine speed was dictated by the size of gear ratio in the machine assembly arms. The gears were replaced with a smaller diameter, increasing the speed of the machine by one fifth.

4. Employees from other areas were cross-trained to replace missing assembly machine operators, thus increasing the ability to exploit the constraint.

The four above improvements sufficiently increased capacity at assembly and the constraint moved to the market.

In 6 months, this plant achieved consistent on-time delivery of 99.9%. In other words, they were shipping 30% more product and uncovered enough excess capacity to ship their current volume in three shifts, 5 days a week vs. the previous four shifts, 7 days a week. They are currently looking at how to use this excess capacity to exploit the marketplace, which brings us to the next issue — what to do with the excess capacity discovered when TOC becomes the way of thinking, acting, and improving.

This company is now faced with two courses of action. Cut the labor force and save roughly one fourth of the direct labor costs or keep the work force and aggressively go after some segment of the market. They are again at the cross-roads of defining themselves as a cost-driven company or a throughput-driven company. The temptation to slip back into cost-minimizing actions and strategies vs. TOC throughput and growth strategies surfaces every time a company successfully completes step four (elevate the constraint). It is at this juncture, when a company does not know how to manage the constraint or the constraint has moved beyond their ability or their perceived ability to manage, that TOC's continuous process of improvement stops. The thought-process tools are most critical now to combine marketing, engineering, operations, and finance to use the competitive edge factor the plant has created and go after the market. The weaving company has experienced phenomenal success in two plants. The constraint has moved to the market, overtime has been eliminated, 99.9% on-time delivery is the standard, cycle time has been reduced by 25% and inventory by 35%, and the plant consistently demonstrates excess capacity of 25%; yet, the company is at its most vulnerable point in the journey. Will they take a one-time 25% labor decrease, ignore market opportunity, and lose the partnership of their workforce to drive improvements? The jury is out on this one. It will either be one of my next book's success chapters or end up in my *Dilbert* stories. There is a predictable outcome to either path.

6 New Manufacturing Floor Measures and Reporting

D
rum-Buffer-Rope (DBR) was designed inside the five-step process, and the five steps are integral to managing the system. Understanding DBR measurements requires an explanation of how to measure and report using the first three steps (identify, exploit, and subordinate). Monitoring the buffers and excess queue at non-drum operations is the basic reporting structure for identifying bottlenecks and focusing subordination efforts of all other resource departments. Monitoring the performance of the drums is the basis of exploitation. A company's ability to exploit the constraint resource is dependent on correct identification of the bottleneck and the ability of the non-drum operations and support functions to subordinate to the care and feeding of the drum.

Theory of Constraints is a thinking process that requires people to make logical decisions based on the current environment using key barometers. Depending on the current environment, the workforce will change its actions to maximize the systems output. For this to be accomplished, the barometer must correctly model the system and reflect the constrained activities of the organization. The people on the floor must understand the model, and they must have the authority to act. The workforce must be able to challenge and explain their actions to themselves and others. To create and sustain an empowered environment requires a common knowledge base and a simple, practical tool kit. DBR provides the model, and the thought process supplies the tool kit.

Ask yourself what an organization really wants from its people. Is it adherence to maximizing a single measure, regardless of the circumstances the work environment is experiencing? Obviously not; that is why the balanced scorecard approach is getting so much attention. Organizations want people to increase quality while controlling or reducing costs and continuously decreasing inventory while achieving 100% on-time delivery. We want it all!

The previous chapters should have convinced you of the conflicts inherent in the previous paragraph. If not, review the spider web of conflict cloud in Chapter 2, Figure 2.2, which details the conflicting actions necessary to maximize the measures designed to ensure maximum quality, cost reduction, on-time delivery, and inventory reduction. You can only achieve the maximum your system can support (the highest return on investment) by understanding and managing the systems constraints. You cannot have more than the physical resource constraints of the organization can generate, but you can certainly have a lot less by not exploiting them.

An empowered workforce must be able to understand conflict in the system, solve the conflict, and communicate the need for action laterally and vertically. The following are examples of how to use DBR and the five-step process to create the barometer and feedback systems. Actual examples of how companies have used clouds to logically diagram different potential actions around exploitation and their solutions are used throughout the chapter. Solutions begin at the lowest level of the organization, the level with the ability to create change through action, and these actions must be tied back to the strategic vision at the top of the organization. Without the ability to change the basic behavior of the organization, the strategic vision, no matter how brilliantly worded, will remain only a plaque decorating the company walls.

Constraint Identification Reporting

One of the best features about DBR scheduling is that if you pick the wrong drum, the right drum will appear because of buffer management. You cannot run the system without knowing you have picked the wrong drum! If the real drum is in front of the scheduled drum, work will be late reaching the scheduled drum, and holes will consistently appear in the buffer due to work queuing in front of the real drum. A hole in the buffer denotes product is not available for the drum schedule.

Consistent holes in the buffer, causing the drum to miss its schedule, can happen because somewhere upstream the real drum is processing parts slower than the scheduled drum. If the real drum is after the scheduled drum, the queue of parts will build continuously at an operation downstream, and holes will appear in the shipping buffer. Queue is inevitable because product is released to the shop at the rate of the scheduled drums. If the release is faster than another operation on the floor, queue will build at the slower operation. This does not mean that every time a queue builds we need to move the drum.

Random strikes by "Murphy" can cause a queue to build at any work sequence, but non-drums should have sufficient capacity to recover. Spikes due to "Murphy" are part of every manufacturing system, and DBR expects them. When a queue builds at an operation, operators need to change their work behavior. Non-drum work priority is usually based on strict first-in, first-out (FIFO) principles, unless an order has been identified as late to a buffer and is being expedited. Strict FIFO principles include not setting product aside to accumulate batches for setup savings. Queue building at an operation alerts the operator of the need to speed up. A possible time-saving course of action is batching like parts in the queue. If queue continues to grow, it is time to call in help. The queuing information dictates where and when to authorize overtime and where to focus process improvement or cross-training efforts.

Monitoring queue on a real-time basis is an essential part of a DBR reporting system. Non-drums with chronic queuing problems will consistently show up in the buffer-management reporting structure as a source of *severe buffer penetration or drum and shipping schedule misses.* Tracking the frequency and cause of severe buffer penetration and drum schedule or shipping schedule misses is the best indicator of operations with insufficient surplus or sprint capacity. An area's ability to sprint or catch up when "Murphy" strikes governs the system's ability to recover time. The less sprint capacity, the more time needs to be reserved in the drum and shipping buffers to ensure drum and shipping schedule integrity. Generally speaking, the less sprint that non-drum operations have, the larger the buffers need to be.

The same rules on exploitation for the drum should be applied to non-drums with chronic queuing. Do not change drums until exploitation principles have been exhausted at the non-drum and elevation considered. Exploitation involves close examination of why the queue is building and is explained at length later in this chapter. Temporary shifts in product mix can cause a temporary bottleneck. If exploitation principles do not sufficiently increase capacity or the change in product mix is long term, consideration must be given to elevating the resource.

Switching the drum to a lower capacity resource will lower the output of total product dependent on the new drum. The drum paces the factory, and a slower pace will mean less throughput. Often elevation can be as simple as changing a work practice, offloading to another resource, batching a particular part, or buying simple tools such as additional gauges. Note, even though we are using the queuing and buffer management reporting to identify new or future bottlenecks, the next steps are exploit and then elevate. Subordination was not mentioned, because the intent was to elevate (increase the capacity of the bottleneck), *not* to move the drum. Subordination was inherent in our decision to elevate. We subordinated our work efforts and investment spending to elevating the bottleneck to create sufficient sprint capacity to exploit the drum. Sprint capacity in front of the drum allows schedule recovery when random disruption happens in front of the drum. There is a tradeoff between investment in sprint and investment in time to recover (the buffer in front of the drum is a way to store time to recover). A company can invest in sprint capacity or work-in-process inventory and longer cycle time to protect the drum.

Exploitation

If the pace of the drum determines the pace of the manufacturing operation, then exploitation of the drum allows the exploitation of the manufacturing operation. This is a basic premise of TOC and DBR. Assuming we have correctly scheduled the realistic capacity of the real drum, the first question around exploitation is "Are we meeting the drum schedule?" Missing the drum schedule creates the potential of missing a shipping date. The first measure at a drum is a measure of on-time performance to the drum schedule. From a practical standpoint, it means tracking completion of shop orders or numbers of parts through the drum in compliance with the scheduled completion. Sliding a drum schedule slides the plant's schedule, pushes out orders, and increases the backlog.

If we are not meeting the schedule, then the second question is "Why are we are missing the schedule?" If the schedule misses are because the material was not available, then there is probably a subordination issue at some operation in front of the drum. Subordination is the basis for 90% of a company's activity, and Chapter 7 is devoted solely to the subject. Exploitation is the focus if the drum schedule is missed because the drum cannot keep the scheduled pace. Finding as little as 10% additional capacity at a drum can translate to an equivalent 10% increase in sales at no additional operating cost.

Some floor managers do not think the savings of staggering breaks and lunches to increase the drum uptime will make an important difference to the plant, but it can add 10% of additional throughput to the operation dependent on the drum. A 10% increase in throughput translates to net profit at a dramatically higher rate than 10%. Throughput is equivalent to sales dollars minus the cost of raw materials and any other truly variable costs (variable costs increase proportionately in a one-to-one ratio with an increase in volume).

Truly variable costs (raw materials and outside manufacturing costs) are usually less than 50% of the cost of goods sold. A $100,000 increase in sales due to a 10% increase in production units leads to a $50,000 increase in net profit if the true variable cost is 50%. Contribution margin is the measure of the economic principles in breakeven analysis that allow a company to leverage off of its fixed costs. Management accounting applies the breakeven economic principles in direct costing. The equation for throughput in management accounting is sales revenue minus variable costs equals the contribution margin of a product. This is the dollar value after covering the variable costs available to contribute to fixed costs. If fixed costs have been covered, the entire contribution margin is available to contribute to increasing the period's net profit.

Maximizing the constraint resource leverages the entire organization's fixed costs. If the constraint resource is a machine, measuring output efficiency and uptime is essential to evaluating the constraint resource exploitation. Constraint resource measures are focused on utilization and efficiency. This should be easy because they are the measures all companies are used to. Here are the basic questions to ask to rate an area on their exploitation effort:

1. Is the machine manned through breaks and lunches?
2. Does the operation lose uptime at shift change?
3. Is an operator or setup person spending time at some other function (paperwork, cleanup, chasing down parts or tools) that reduces their ability to keep the resource running?
4. Is there a machine/operation/skilled person who can relieve some of the drum's workload?
5. What is causing the drum downtime, and can we find a way to stop or decrease the downtime?
6. Where and how can I increase capacity at the drum, and who can do it?
7. Do I have any parts that could run on other, "less-efficient" equipment but which have been scheduled through this center because it is the best practice or takes less setup time or provides the least-cost part? Sometimes our best practices or unit cost ideas mislead us. If there is older equipment that is qualified and has idle time available, and we choose not to use it because it takes longer to set up or run, we are artificially limiting the entire plant. We have just missed the opportunity for the company to ship more product and make more money.
8. Is there adequate skilled backup to allow for exploitation?
9. Is there a vendor we could outsource for drum parts to increase the plant's capacity?

The following example of one of my clients clearly demonstrates the difficulty in making the shift from cost-world thinking to throughput-world thinking regarding exploitation of the constraint vs. exploiting unit labor cost. The company is an aerospace division of a multi-billion dollar Fortune 500 company. They chose TOC and DBR as a potential solution to increase their on-time delivery which had been hovering at 60%. I became involved with the company two months after they had implemented a finite-scheduling package designed around DBR principles. The company had not addressed the culture and measurement changes required to create the understanding to manage with DBR successfully. Although the scheduling package identified the drums

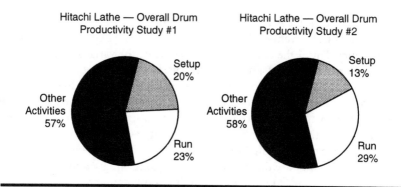

Hitachi Lathe — Overall Drum
Productivity Study #1

Setup
20%

Other
Activities
57%

Run
23%

Hitachi Lathe — Overall Drum
Productivity Study #2

Setup
13%

Other
Activities
58%

Run
29%

Figure 6.1. Drum Productivity Studies

and scheduled the rate of flow through the plant at the pace of the drums, the drum environment was managed with the previous Manufacturing Resource Planning (MRP) mentality and cost measures.

The drums consistently and continually failed to meet their schedule. Failing to meet a drum schedule ultimately means failing to meet the shipping schedule. In the weekly planning sessions, the finite scheduler would consistently push out the ship date for the orders the drum failed to complete. The improved shipping performance was not materializing. The drum area managers insisted they understood exploitation and laid the blame for the failure to make schedule on the increased number of setups. Smaller batch sizes with increased numbers of setups were based on scheduling end-item demand requirements rather than the previous large MRP batch sizes designed to minimize setups. The area managers also insisted the standards used to schedule the drums were unrealistic, even though the standards had been based on actual past-performance run times. I insisted the problem was a lack of exploitation and wanted them to address the nine questions to resolve exploitation. They insisted the drums were working as fast as they could, and the problem was in the schedule batch sizes and unrealistic run times. They wanted to increase the batch sizes. We were stalemated, and plant performance was deteriorating. We used the cloud process and agreed that one of us had flawed assumptions. Our solution was to have industrial engineering conduct a series of random productivity observation studies at the drums and settle the question of how the drums spent their day.

The study was centered on two of the drums. The first study covered a 4-day time period and the second a 5-day time period. The remarkably similar results added credibility to the study. The results for both of the drum studies are illustrated in a pie chart in Figure 6.1. For the Hitachi lathe in the figure, setups were nearly equal to the run time in the first study and half the run time in the second study, so setup and batch size clearly were not the problem. In both studies, downtime for the lathe was 57% and 58%, respectively. More than half of the time the drum was not running or was in setup. In the first study, 22% of the 57% machine downtime was due to the operator being out of the area (including breaks and lunches), and 37% involved the operator running a non-drum resource in the area. In the second study, 31% of the 58% machine downtime was due to the operator being out of the area. For an additional 15% of the downtime, the operator was running a non-drum resource in the area, and for another 15% the setup was being held while waiting for additional parts to create larger batches and avoid additional setups. The study clearly showed the drum was not being exploited. More importantly, it demonstrated to management what assumptions were driving actions on the shop floor. The assumptions clearly showed the choices made were designed around saving and exploiting labor cost, not exploiting the bottleneck machine utilization and maximizing output. The study showed that setups and batch size were not the problem. The operators being pulled off to run other operations, leaving the lathes unattended during breaks and lunches, and holding setups to wait for additional parts were the reasons for the drum schedule misses. The lathes were not being exploited.

The necessity of changing the past practice of exploiting labor and setups by having one operator run multiple machines was evident. Because the lathes were the constraining resource, holding the machine idle for parts to arrive to save an additional setup may be a good decision. If the idle time was less than setup time saved, the decision would maximize our ability to exploit the machine. It was not a good decision if the idle time was less than the setup time. In my client's case, the idle-time study revealed that operator availability was responsible for the majority of the drum downtime, and the downtime exceeded combined run and setup time.

Based on the results of the study, it was evident that to exploit the drum's additional labor resources, they would need to be available at the drum; more importantly, however, shop-floor management would need to change its view of what and how to exploit. Total direct labor as a percentage of cost of sales was less than 8%. If the drum dictated the pace of the entire plant, and the plant was at less than 60% on-time delivery, and backlog was growing, then increasing uptime at the drum would increase throughput. The labor increase added less than .1% to total cost but increased throughput at the drum by 25%. This particular drum was responsible for producing parts that were needed on 60% of the products the plant produced. Based on the work done at two of the drums, the other six drums adopted the measurement and evaluation system pioneered by the first study. Machine uptime was tracked based on a series of ten codes designed to capture major reasons for downtime.

The same exploitation practices for drums should be applied to areas with little or no sprint capacity. Buffer management should expose areas where product consistently queues and causes holes in either drum buffers or shipping buffers. Before an area is considered for classification as a drum or is elevated through investment, the area should be examined for opportunities to exploit. The same questions for exploitation and the thinking process (TP) logical diagrams of conflict (clouds) can be applied with amazing success. This is the basis for a continuous improvement model around TOC. Focusing improvement to exploit the constraining resources and increase sprint capacity where necessary ensures the highest return on improvement investments. Actions at the drums must be based on exploitation. Giving the people running the drum the ability to use clouds to challenge their own and each other's actions and assumptions is critical to their ability to make and communicate good action decisions.

Exploitation is not just for the drum but is also essential thinking for any area with insufficient sprint capacity (capacity over the drum capacity sufficient to recover from "Murphy"). If a resource area is consistently causing red zone holes or misses at the drum or shipping schedule, we need to increase capacity at that resource. Exploitation examples can be applied to either the drum or a non-drum resource, causing consistent holes in the buffer and endangering the drum or shipping schedule.

Predictably, a company's view of best practice or minimizing unit cost can get in the way of good exploitation decisions. A common example occurs when an older piece of equipment is replaced or supplemented with a faster, tighter tolerance machine. The faster, better machine is either a drum or is a piece of equipment with very little sprint capacity. The new machine is viewed as the best practice because it minimizes setup, produces more parts per hour, and has tighter tolerances than the old machine. One of the easiest ways to increase capacity is to offload product to another resource. What is the effect if we offload some of the faster machine load to the old machine? What factors should we consider before we make the decision? What is the impact on throughput? What is the impact on true cost (cash out the door)? What is the impact on unit cost measures, and is unit cost a valid consideration? How would we have made the decision in the past? The thought-process tool to examine the two potential courses of action is the cloud.

The answers to the above questions form the basis for the assumptions surrounding the logic of choosing to offload to the slower machine or to wait for availability on the new, faster machine and the predicted effect on return on investment. The cloud in Figure 6.2 was constructed to consider offloading work from the new, faster resource to the old machine and is read A to B to D as follows: To exploit return on investment, I must increase total throughput. To increase total throughput, I must offload work to the old machine. A to C to D' is read as follows: To exploit return on investment, I must make the best use of resources. To make the best use of resources, I must wait for availability on the new machine.

Assumptions are the glue holding logic together. Our conclusions are only as good as the assumptions on which they are based. Understanding the assumptions allows the logic of the desired actions to be challenged openly. The

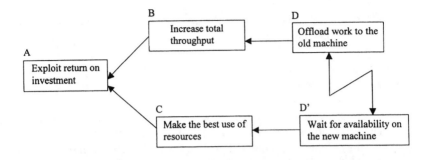

Figure 6.2. Offloading the Constraint Conflict Cloud

assumption underlying the B-D arrow is that to increase total throughput, I must offload to the old machine because:

1. The old machine is process capable for some products.
2. Product run on the old machine increases total plant output by offloading the bottleneck.
3. Total lead-time for product using these parts will be reduced.
4. Increase in labor to run the old machines is less than the increase in throughput dollars (sales dollars – raw materials dollars).
5. Running the old machine will not negatively impact the new machine (steal resources or scarce labor necessary to exploit the new machine).
6. The old machine has idle time available for setups and run time of parts to be offloaded from the new machine.

The assumption underlying the C-D' arrows is that to make the best use of resources, I must wait for the availability of the new machine because:

1. The new machine takes less time to set up.
2. The new machine takes less time to run the part.
3. The new machine has tighter tolerance capability.
4. The old machine is not in the routing.
5. We do not have enough skilled labor to set up both machines.

By failing to offload to the old machine, they were limiting the entire plant's output to the output of the new machine. The assumptions are true, but they are irrelevant if the objective is to increase the bottom line and make the best use of the entire plant as a resource investment base. Even if only 15% of the parts were approved as process capable on the old machine, the entire output of the product lines dependent on the drum could increase by 15%. In this particular case, the throughput increase or bottom-line impact was $13.5

million. The actions and decisions at the drum could clearly be measured and traced to a bottom-line impact. The increase at the drum increased total plant throughput.

The assumptions exposed in regard to deciding to wait for the new machine to be available are the assumptions that increasing labor cost or setups (both of which are examples of minimizing unit cost) makes the best use of resources. The best use of resources is to maximize the shippable product for the entire plant. The extra setups on the old machine are free from a capacity standpoint, because if the old machine has idle time then spending capacity in setup has no cost. There is no lost opportunity! If the setup of the old machine cannot be accomplished with existing labor, then the cost of the additional person added to run the old machine is the only relevant cost in the decision to offload to the old machine. If the increase in throughput dollars (sales dollars less variable costs dollars) gained is greater than the cost of adding a person, then net profit will increase due to the decision to offload. If net profit increases and there is no additional investment (the old machine was idle), then return on investment increases.

The decision to exploit labor rather than machine output would *only* be correct if the plant's constraint is skilled labor. This is assumption #5 under the C-D' arrow. If operating the old machine caused the new machine to sit idle because of a scarce labor resource and the new machine had a higher output per labor unit, we would need to increase our skilled labor pool (step four in TOC is to elevate the constraint) or only run the new machine in order to exploit the skilled labor resource. Until the time that additional labor could be acquired, the scarce labor resource should be exploited to create the greatest output per unit of labor. We should wait for availability of the new, faster machine to run the parts. This should be a temporary decision until we can elevate the labor resource (step four in TOC is to elevate).

Note that the cloud clearly shows it is not always right or always wrong to offload to the old machine. The assumptions surrounding the current reality determine the best course of action to exploit return on investment. By exposing the assumptions around which action to take and what need the action fulfills, we can make the best decision in the current reality. Based upon all of the assumptions, except #5, under the C-D' arrow (we do not have enough skilled labor to set up both machines), the best decision is to offload to the old machine. If assumption #5 is true, then we should use the scarce labor resource to exploit the faster machine. The drum area manager of a client created this cloud. The whole solution increased drum capacity by over 25% and included a second cloud regarding how to elevate the labor pool.

When considering how to elevate the resource, a cloud can be used to explore the necessity of having to hire an additional skilled machinist. One of the assumptions about the necessity of hiring additional skilled labor was that current machinists were spending all of their time working on setups or troubleshooting, both of which required a high skill level. If that assumption was flawed, then a potential solution would be to hire a helper for the skilled machinist and offload work to the helper. For example, if a skilled machinist, essential for machine setup and troubleshooting, is spending time on clerical paperwork, cleanup, routine quality checks, handling parts, or other unskilled tasks, then their ability to exploit the constraint machine uptime is reduced. By offloading their unrelated work to a lesser skilled individual, assumption #5 can be invalidated. This could free enough time for the setup and troubleshooting to be performed on both machines. In my client's case, hiring helpers at $10 per hour rather than machinists at $30 per hour broke the cloud.

Exploitation through offloading the skilled labor resource might even negate the need for additional skilled labor or additional capital investment in more machinery. Note that at no time are we concerned with exploiting the cost of labor. We are concerned with exploiting the labor unit of work output. Productivity at the drum is defined as good output per resource unit of time. In order to exploit machine uptime, it is necessary to understand why a machine is down and then take steps to decrease the downtime. Increasing machine uptime may be as simple as covering breaks and lunches, keeping a set of tools or gauges at each machine, hiring labor to unload parts, staging work at the machine center, completing shop paperwork, or doing area cleanup.

There is a clear difference between cost-world thinking and measures and throughput-world thinking and measures. In a throughput world, we are not exploiting labor cost; instead, we are exploiting the constraining machine resource or operation output. This means exploiting the labor content centered around the constraining resource. We may want to increase our total labor outlay by hiring an additional direct labor resource if it increases our ability to generate throughput at a greater rate than increased cost. A throughput increase at the constraint translates directly to net profit.

It is baffling to me why American business is willing to increase the total fixed investment cost base with an automated machine costing $250,000 but is unwilling to hire a labor resource with an annual cost of $25,000 to exploit the new automation gain. By focusing on minimizing labor, companies often fail to capitalize on their investment. Worse yet, they waste their investment dollars by elevating resources that have not been exploited because of poor labor utilization decisions.

Does return on investment go up with the above actions and solutions? Yes! With direct labor as 8% of sales dollars, a 12.5% increase in direct labor would add only 1% to cost of goods sold. The real question is what it would add to the throughput dollars of the company. If we were able to ship our current backlog, decrease our overtime expense, decrease our cycle time (and, therefore, our work-in-process inventory), it would be money well spent. The key to any investment decision is to focus the additions to exploit the drums and to increase sprint capacity in areas having insufficient sprint capacity to protect the drums or shipping schedules. Labor is an investment. Equipment is an investment. DBR is a focus tool to reveal where and how to exploit the company's investment dollars. In the particular example above, the plant hired two additional helpers at $10 per hour. The total plant head count was just under 700 employees, and the increase in throughput dollar potential was over $13 million.

7 New Measures for Operations: Subordination

The ability to subordinate will define a company's ability to succeed with the Theory of Constraints. Exploitation of the constraint is dependent on effective subordination. Without a clear understanding of subordination, the non-drums will create conflict with themselves and others regarding their action-priority decisions and resource allocation. Successful subordination requires all non-constraint resources to understand their relationship to the constraint and to define their actions by the impact the action will have on exploiting the constraint. When applying Drum-Buffer-Rope (DBR), all non-drums must understand their role to support the constraint and the impact of their actions on both the drum and shipping schedules and buffers. Conflict causes disruption. Disruption causes waste and the accumulations of delays. Delays and waste cause costs to go up and throughput to go down. Successful subordination is dependent on the quick resolution of conflict and communication of the resolution to align actions to ensure that the constraining resources are protected from disruption. Minimizing conflict minimizes disruption and wasted time, providing more time that can be used to increase throughput.

Over the last three years, I have developed a methodology for teaching an organization to create subordination rules and definitions to align work priority in all work areas by using DBR. I use the movie *The Goal,* which is about 45 minutes long and can be viewed any time before the training begins. The movie gives a good basic overview of TOC and DBR concepts and provides a common basis of knowledge for those participating in the training program. I spend the first hour of training reiterating the basic concepts of DBR and TOC, using the following material.

Review of the Basics

Drum-Buffer-Rope revolves around five principles defined by the five-step process of TOC:

1. A system can be managed from the identifiable resources constraining the system.
2. Scheduling and exploiting the use of the constraining resources exploits the system.
3. Buffering protects the constraining resources from disruptions downstream and ensures the ability to exploit.
4. All non-constraining resources must subordinate to these critical areas; in other words, take actions to ensure that there is no disruption in the ability to exploit the constraining resource. Therefore, there must be enough spare (sprint) capacity at the non-constraining resources to ensure that they can recover from random disruption and temporary queues due to a temporary product-mix change and continue to protect the flow of work to the constraints.
5. Elevation of the constraining resource elevates the capacity of the entire system; elevation of non-drum resources with insufficient sprint capacity ensures the ability to exploit the constraining resource.

The five steps of TOC define the five principles and describe how to improve the system continuously:

1. Identify the constraints (pick the control points for the system based on strategy or physical capacity).
2. Exploit the constraint (schedule the best use). The measurement for exploitation is resource utilization efficiency, and the manager of the drum is measured on exploitation. Buffers safeguard the ability to exploit.
3. Subordinate all other resources to the decision to exploit the constraint resource. (All other resource managers' ability to subordinate is measured by the buffer, on-time rope release, and work-in-process queues.)
4. Elevate the constraining resource.
5. Start over and identify the new constraining resource.

All areas in the company, other than the drums, are measured on their subordination efforts. Buffer management and tracking of the constraining resources and shipping buffers, on-time release of raw materials, and queuing at nondrums provide the tools and reporting to measure subordination of operations feeding the buffers. Any area in the organization can cause the drum or shipping to miss the schedule.

In DBR, the drum is the constraining resource. The drum's pace sets the schedule and the work priority for the entire shop. The buffer is a pocket of time, reserved in front of the constraining resource and in front of the shipping date, designed to protect the due dates of the drum schedule and the shipping schedule. Our ability to hit the scheduled date for the drum to run and the date to ship to our customers is dependent on two things:

1. The size of the buffer is large enough to allow for variable unscheduled activities ("Murphys") in front of the buffer. The time to recover buffer depletion is dependent on excess capacity (sprint capacity) that can be cranked up when the buffer is penetrated. The ability to sprint guards the ability to exploit.
2. The release of raw material is on time to support work arriving in the buffers to support the drum's scheduled run time and the shipping schedule due date.

The length of time necessary to accomplish the processes and buffers in front of the drum and the ship date determine the necessary release date to support the drum and shipping schedules. This is known as the rope in DBR. The rope length is dependent on the time of the processes in front of the buffer and the buffer time. If plant exploitation is dependent on exploitation of the drum, and exploitation of the drum is dependent on the buffer, then on-time release at the first processes and subsequent part indenture levels is a necessary condition to ensure plant exploitation.

Sprinting (working as fast as you can when you have work) at non-drums and transferring work in time (transfer at the end of a specific time period, regardless of units available), rather than batch transfer, ensures work flows through the plant with minimum cycle time. Transferring work in time, rather than batch, minimizes the starve/flood cycles common at assembly and test areas due to transferring in fixed batch sizes.

Sprint capacity is defined as the capacity that an area has available in excess of the drum capacity. Sprint ability defines the ability an area has to recover from any "Murphy" (late parts, machine downtime, operator absence, and quality rework problems). The more sprint ability, the less buffer time is needed to ensure exploitation of the drum.

There is a direct dollar tradeoff between investing in capacity to sprint faster to create buffer or investing in inventory to create buffer to protect the constraining resources and shipping schedules. The biggest tradeoff is often cycle time. A buffer of two days of work in process may be sufficient protection if the operations in front of the drum have 40% excess capacity over the drum. A buffer of 5 days may be necessary if the sprint capacity upstream from the drum is only 15% greater than the drum.

An additional important tradeoff in cycle time comes from the decisions around transfer batches. The rate of flow of product through the shop is a major determining factor in cycle time. Product can be transferred based on a batch size or based on time increments. Transferring in time increments means all parts finished at the end of a designated time period (e.g., every hour, shift, or day) are transferred to the next operation. Transferring by batch means all parts will wait until the batch is finished before moving to the next operation. The smaller the transfer batch, the more the cycle time should shrink. Allowing inventory to pool in batches before transfer increases the flood/starve or python effect common to manufacturing operations. Large batch transfer is one of the ways to create the appearance of a floating bottleneck. Total cycle time dramatically increases when work in process is transferred in larger batches vs. smaller time increments. Keeping batches intact through the transfer process is a common practice based on the belief that the extra setups required for small transfer batches waste capacity and cause "costs" to increase. Setups at non-constraints are "free" under the TOC philosophy. Remember, cost is defined as cash outflow or lost opportunity for throughput (cash inflow); it is not an account for the allocation of fixed costs. The valuation of setups was explored in depth in Chapter 4.

Measuring subordination is difficult but is the key to TOC success. First we must design metrics that track and encourage the system to start on time, and we must also create the flexibility to allow the system and metrics to evolve as changes or new realizations in the environment occur. The measure of how and when subordination has failed is accomplished through buffer management, monitoring on-time release of parts to the floor, and monitoring areas where "Murphy" has struck and recovery help is needed (evidenced by increasing queues or holes in the buffer). These areas are critical gates through which inventory must pass so that we can track work in process effectively without micro-managing the system. A good analogy is the use of "waypoints" or checkstations by the military when they are coordinating the movement of large groups of people and vehicles and there is no visibility. Any area of the company can cause a hole in the buffer by not completing and passing the correct work on quickly. A miss in the drum schedule or the shipping schedule can be caused by the failure to understand how to prioritize support for manufacturing and or by working parts in the wrong priority to support the decision to exploit the drums or the shipping schedule.

Holes in the buffer reveal the potential for a missed schedule. Holes that repeatedly are caused by the same issue or area are used to focus attention and extra resources to the area in danger of or repeatedly causing a hole. Roles and responsibilities designed around subordination need to be clearly understood, and the visibility to support or subordinate to helping other areas is essential. Metrics to support the actions required for subordination need to be created; metrics that interfere or encourage the wrong actions need to be removed. TOC is a focus tool, and DBR is part of the tool set. Buffer management is a tool that needs an instruction set, a gauge (measures), and training in every area. Buffer management and subordination are how we tie the front end of the business to the back end and link everything in between.

Under systems scheduled with Manufacturing Resource Planning (MRP) software, work-in-process inventory is scattered throughout the manufacturing floor, buffering the organization's resources from "Murphy" everywhere. The good news is we can avoid dealing with our conflicts and compromises because the excess inventory hides the core problems. The bad news is we have a very long cycle time and the only answer to all conflicts and compromises is to learn to become very good expediters. This is an expensive and wasteful system. Missing the rope release date by a week requires using sprint capacity to recover the drum and shipping schedule or creating excess buffer to cover the late release. One of our clients referred to this as the "scramble system".

Using TOC, the excess work in process (buffers of time being everywhere) is gone, replaced with strategic buffers of time in front of constraining resources and shipping. The good news is that cycle time is short, and expediting is the exception and focused at very specific issues and times. The bad news is that your unresolved conflict areas are uncovered and must be dealt with. The inability to resolve the old core conflicts has broken down many DBR implementations in the past. Conflicts over where to place resources, how to prioritize work, and metrics to monitor work outcomes must be aligned. The conflicts are the same old chronic conflicts that have plagued the system forever. How do we prioritze work, process improvement, and capital investment when everything appears equally important and everyone in the system is competing for scarce resources? The company and its people are no longer able to avoid solving them. If the mechanism to let people solve the conflict is not provided, the improvement initiative will get lost in their frustration at being set up to fail.

An organization will ultimately define its success by how well it can resolve conflict. Clouds are conflict-resolution tools designed to give yourself and others clarity regarding the issues and to find practical solutions that ensure that the conditions necessary to achieve the overall return on investment are protected. The balance of this chapter is designed to teach a company how to achieve what appears to be impossible by providing win-win solutions for local actions aligned with return on investment (ROI) for the organization as a whole. The material and methodology used in this chapter's example were designed to take an MRP environment in the aerospace industry and restructure operations into a TOC environment.

After establishing the DBR and TOC basics, the next step is to help the work group translate the generic knowledge to their own environment. Having the group build their own reference environment is critical to establish their understanding about using DBR as the TOC focus tool to prioritize work and expose the negative consequences of working any other priority.

Translating the generic knowledge they have learned into their own environment requires that each area define where they fit in the simple flow diagram shown in Figure 7.1. They must also identify how their actions impact

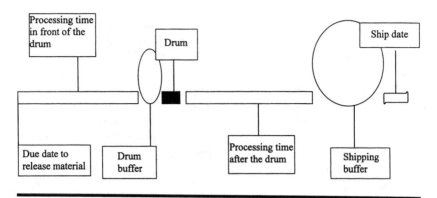

Figure 7.1. Four Key Measurement Visibility Points in a DBR System

the four key measurement/visibility points: time release of raw materials, queue building at non-drums, on-time delivery to the drum buffer, and on-time delivery to the shipping buffer. Some areas will impact only one directly; some will impact all four. Receiving Inspection clearly impacts the rope release date directly. Missing the rope release date jeopardizes all of the buffers and schedules and requires an expedite response through all plant sequences. This is a very disruptive and expensive solution requiring either high sprint investment or large buffers.

The Reference Environment

I have found the use of a reference environment helpful in making the transition from theory to practice. The following reference environment was the Receiving Inspection department of a large aerospace plant at the time of the DBR subordination training. Receiving Inspection had roughly 4 days' worth of queue, and their average process time was 2.8 days (the spread of material aging varied from 1 day to 20 days). Their target work metric was 2.0 days of average queue time. Some of the material inspected would end up going to Quality for disposition. Quality will send some back to the supplier (and Purchasing will be involved in replacing the material), some material will require Engineering's approval for use, and some will be sent to an internal process for rework before it can be received. Material passing inspection will be processed through Stores and released to the floor to begin processing. Fifty percent of all material receipts are late per the release due date established by the DBR scheduling system, and much of the remaining material is months ahead of the scheduled due date release to the floor.

Everyone has a different view of the priority each of the areas should assign to its work. Interspersed are program or brand managers, each concerned with ensuring that the raw material necessary for their programs receives attention immediately. Individual program managers were defining what should be expedited. Each area was attempting to process the work in front of them in the best manner and achieve their area's work metrics. They were each focused on achieving their local optima metric, defined in our original cost world vs. throughput world cloud (Figure 2.9). The new DBR scheduling assigned a window of time for material to be released to the floor:

1. Don't do before (DDB) date — Do not release this to the floor before this date or you will cause resources to work the wrong priority.
2. Expedite — if you have not released the material by this date, expedite the material to get it released (some percentage of the buffer has eroded).

All areas responsible for resolving the release issues of raw material can cause further erosion of the buffer and endanger the ability to exploit shipping on time by not subordinating their work priority to the two dates above.

Identifying the Metric Conflict and Aligning Priority

The training group identified the new DBR work priority as the oldest items past the expedite date and then prioritized work by the most current DDB date. The obvious prioritization of actions necessary to support the manufacturing schedule did not match up with the old work actions necessary to support the area metrics of Receiving, Receiving Inspection, Stores, Planning, Purchasing, and Design Engineering. The metric for these areas was common across manufacturing and based on minimizing aging. The action priority of minimizing aging is to work the item first that was received first (first-in, first-out, or FIFO).

The work group identified the obvious conflict and constructed a cloud based on logically diagramming the action necessary to fulfill the current metric and the action necessary to subordinate to releasing the correct material to the floor on time. The A-B-D side of the cloud in Figure 7.2 is read as follows: To maximize throughput dollars, we must subordinate our actions to support the drum and shipping schedules. To subordinate our actions to support the drums and shipping schedules, we must prioritize work items based on their due date to the floor. The A-C-D' of the cloud is read as follows: To maximize throughput dollars, we must maximize our work outcomes by minimizing aging in our area. To maximize our work outcome and minimize aging in our area, we must work parts in the order they were received (FIFO).

The assumption under the B-D arrow can be stated: To subordinate to the drum and shipping schedules, we must prioritize work items based on their due date to the floor because:

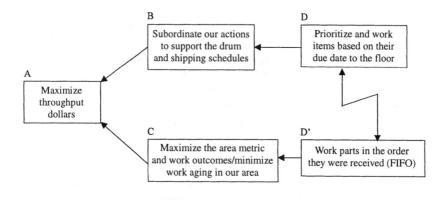

Figure 7.2. Conflict Cloud To Establish New Measures To Support the New DBR Environment

1. Missing the rope release endangers drum and shipping schedules.
2. Missing the rope release erodes the buffers.
3. Buffers are designed to address a "Murphy" on the floor, not late release.
4. Late release will cause a part to be expedited through the shop.
5. Some parts are needed before others, regardless of when they arrive.
6. An order's due date is visible to the floor.

Assumptions under the C-D' arrow can be stated: To maximize the area metric and work outcomes and minimize work aging, we must work parts in the order they were received because:

1. We must move all items through receiving and inspection quickly.
2. FIFO ensures timely completion of paperwork, allowing discounts to be taken with payment.
3. All items have the same priority.
4. We do not have agreement on what is a priority item.

If the action identified as being necessary to ensure subordination is in conflict with the action identified by the current metric, people are immediately faced with a conflict. Should they take actions to ensure their metric or take actions to support subordinating to the company's objective of shipping on time using DBR scheduling? Unless the conflict is resolved and the metric aligned with the desired action required for subordination, the area will either receive unfavorable ratings or fail to support material arriving on time to the floor to ensure timely rope release.

Assumptions 3 and 4 under the C-D' arrow were challenged by Receiving Inspection: Create reporting that first prioritizes material due to be released within 10 days to the floor, sorted by the oldest due date first. The second level of reporting priority was sorted by remaining parts received with discounts available over $50, and the third sort prioritized all remaining parts based on the date the part was received in Stores on a FIFO basis. Their solution both supported the fastest rope release to the floor and saved the company money by taking purchase discounts and ensuring timely completion of remaining work. The solution established expedite priority outside the program manager's sphere of influence.

Metrics and work outcomes were aligned to support the new priorities, and, for the first time all year, Receiving Inspection was able to hit its metric, make the discounts, and get priority work from dock to floor in 1 day vs. 5. The accomplishment of achieving a 1-day dock to floor for late-release materials required coordinating Receiving, Receiving Inspection, Production Control, Planning, and Stores to create a visible fast lane for parts late to the floor.

Receiving, Receiving Inspection, Planning, Production Control, and Stores aligned their work priority and subordinated their own resources to help each other when one area was in danger of not finishing the expedite categories necessary for on-time rope release. Their solution demonstrated their understanding of the following principles regarding subordination:

1. All of the areas involved recognized the need to float their sprint capacity between the departments to support the timely release of materials.
2. Materials missing the rope release date jeopardize the drum and ship schedules.
3. Manufacturing support functions that fail to meet the scheduled release of materials negatively impact the ability to exploit the drum.
4. Much of the accumulated overtime spending throughout the manufacturing sequence was an attempt to catch up to protect shipping due dates and was directly tied to missing rope releases.
5. A better course of action than overtime and expediting was to focus solutions or manpower at the areas to ensure on-time release of materials.
6. Focusing manpower correctly and strategic alignment of action and inventory are more cost-effective solutions than overtime and expediting.

In the above example, simply realigning the metrics and work priorities to support the manufacturing drum schedule reduced the time late items took to get to the floor from 5 days to 1. In this particular case, 50% of incoming items were already late to the manufacturing schedule. The majority of the other 50% of incoming materials was not due for a month or more. In addition, the average queuing of all material in Receiving Inspection dropped from 2.8 days to 1.5 days, and discounts missed decreased significantly. Receiving, Receiving Inspection, Production Control, Stores, and Planning had aligned metrics dependent on taking action to help each other to achieve on-time rope release. Each area could clearly see what work could wait and what work required immediate subordination from another area.

The above solution was designed by the people working in Receiving Inspection in less than 2 hours and implemented in less than 1 week. Receiving Inspection presented the solution to Receiving, Stores, Production Control, and Management Information Systems to gain their input, buy-in, and cooperation. The following facilitation format was developed to guide the Receiving Inspection group through redefining their roles, responsibilities, measures, and reporting requirements based on subordination within a TOC organization. The format is designed to facilitate any non-drum resource's understanding and ability to identify the changes necessary inside their culture and infrastructure to support subordination.

The starting point of such a presentation is making certain that the group understands the generic key concepts around TOC and their environment's application of DBR. After some basic training in concepts, the following question-and-answer format can be used to reiterate the key concepts. The first 11 questions are answered for the group, restating the training basics and reinforcing the DBR scheduling flow diagram (Figure 5.1). The group then answers questions 12 through 21. This procedure accomplishes two basic training essentials. First, people in the group show that they can translate the concept to their own area, and, second, their conflict resolution solutions can be drawn with clouds to introduce them to the concept of logical diagrams of conflict.

1. *What is the Theory of Constraints?* It is a five-step process to maximize the output of any dependent event system. The steps are
   a. Identify the system's constraints.
   b. Exploit the constraints.
   c. Subordinate other processes in the organization to the decision to exploit the constraint.
   d. Elevate the constraint (break it by increasing its ability to perform).
   e. Start over and find the next constraint.
2. *What is Drum-Buffer-Rope (DBR)?* DBR is a method of scheduling manufacturing plants based on identifying the resources that constrain the plant's output. By scheduling and managing the constraining resources, the plant can manage the entire operation using exploitation and subordination techniques described in the five-step TOC process.
3. *What is a drum?* A drum is a strategic operation that has limited resources and determines the flow of work through the system. A system can go only as fast as the slowest or most overloaded resource. This is called the constraining resource, and we use the second step of TOC (exploitation) at the drum.

4. *What is a buffer?* A buffer is a pocket of time represented by work in process which is reserved in front of the drum, the constraining resource, and the shipping due date. The buffer is to protect the due dates of the drum schedule and the shipping schedule. Buffers protect the ability to keep the drums from starving and give a protective cushion to ensure on-time shipping.

5. *What is the rope?* The rope is the length of time necessary to accomplish processes in front of the drum or ship dates. Quantifying the time necessary to complete the processes in front of drums and shipping establishes the necessary release date to support the drum and shipping schedules.

6. *How do we measure the drum?* Exploitation.

7. *How do we measure the rope release performance?* Monitor on-time releases to the schedule to support the drum schedule and or non-drum operations to support the shipping schedule. This is part of subordination.

8. *How do we know the rope is the right length?* Parts arrive inside the buffer times at the buffers in front of the drums and shipping. Parts arriving early or late to the buffer reveal a problem in performing to the rope length.

9. *What is a hole in the buffer?* A hole represents a shop order not arriving in the scheduled time frame. If the buffer is 40 hours, then the shop order can arrive anytime in the 5 days and still be on time, but its absence will be noted by a hole in the buffer until it arrives. If the shop order arrives on the third day, the hole would have been visible for the first 3 days.

10. *How do we measure everyone else's performance to support DBR?* Subordination tracked by on-time material release to the floor and support of the drum/shipping schedule tracked by buffer management at the drum buffer and the shipping buffer. The longer work waits in an area to be worked, the farther the part will penetrate into the buffer. Tracking holes in the buffer to root causes or areas with queues reveals areas in the shop in need of subordination; the improvement process should be focused here. Send resources, improve fixtures and training, reduce setups, offload to other areas — whatever is needed to increase flow. Subordinate as an organization to make sure this area gets the help they need.

11. *What is sprint capacity?* Sprint capacity is an area's ability to catch themselves up when they get behind and send help to other areas to catch up. Areas with excess sprint subordinate to helping others exploit their areas when they are behind. Sprint capacity defines an area's ability to recover from a typical "Murphy" (late parts, machine downtime, operator absence, quality rework problems).

12. How does my area know what our role is in subordination (supporting) to achieve material release schedules and to fill the buffers and

      what our work priorities are, including where to send our excess sprint capacity and exploiting the drums?

13. What visibility do we need in our area to know when high-priority work enters our area?

14. What reporting or tool will we use in our area to align our work priorities with subordinating to the manufacturing floor schedule and ultimately on-time delivery to the market?

After the group answers questions 12, 13, and 14, it is time for the trainer to reveal reporting (prepared ahead of time) that meets the visibility requirements the group has specified when they answered these three questions. If the trainer has not designed some potential reporting, he or she will use the current reporting system to raise questions about how and what needs to be improved to gain the visibility they require. The group will then address how they would create visibility in their areas and ways to visibly recognize when they should subordinate to helping other areas based on work priority. They will also discuss finding ways to measure or reward subordination when the work priority necessitates shifting resources.

15. What metric will my area use to know we are doing a good job of subordinating?

Question 15 prompts thinking about what measures would support the subordination actions discussed previously. This is a good starting point for building a cloud that describes the conflict between their new action or metric and their old action or metric (the above example regarding Receiving Inspection can be used). Receiving Inspection chose to measure the number of items that missed the release date to the floor, and they were also responsible for making sure the company received discounts. A determination of the number of items that missed their discount dates was included in their measurement. Another metric to track was the number of items penetrating the drum buffer and jeopardizing the drum schedule due to items aging in Receiving Inspection. These measurement examples can be used as a reference environment for the group to create measures to ensure their cloud's necessary condition of subordination to the drum and shipping schedules.

16. How well do the current metric and work outcomes of our area fit with subordination?

17. What if the actions I need to take in my area to subordinate to the manufacturing floor schedules are different than the actions needed to achieve my area's measure?

Questions 16 and 17 ask the group to evaluate their old metric and work outcomes against the subordination actions they have identified. If they cannot come up with an existing metric in their area, they will discuss how they determine if they are doing a good job and will use their "good job" definition as the old metric. Use of the cloud establishes what the priority of work would have been under the old metric vs. the work priority under the new subordination actions identified. The actions are written in the opposing action boxes (D and D') using the cloud template (in Figure 7.4), and the conflict is revealed. The group identifies why they need to take each of the actions, and they fill in the B and C boxes on the cloud template with the need for each action. They have just identified their first conflict cloud.

18. What if the actions I need to take in my area to subordinate to the manufacturing floor schedule are different than the actions requested by another area or manager?
19. How do I make a decision about which actions to take when we have a conflict over setting priorities around subordination?

Questions 18 and 19 show how useful the cloud is in solving conflicts and aligning priorities without labeling anyone as being wrong, as the cloud emphasizes the win-win nature of the situation and the common objective of both sides. The group will produce examples of issues raised in questions 18 and 19 and will incorporate these ideas in clouds. It is important to note that if the group can identify the conflict within the cloud but cannot achieve resolution among themselves, they need to show the cloud to their supervisor for resolution or seek facilitation from the TOC internal expert. They should be encouraged to solve the conflict first by themselves. Sample clouds can help. A good example is the "don't turn non-bottlenecks into a bottleneck" cloud. The group must be certain that the action identified as desirable for subordination will produce the desired outcome of the new measurement.

20. How do we fit in other needs the company has with the need to subordinate our actions to the manufacturing floor schedule? (In the Receiving Inspection example, Receiving Inspection needs to ensure the company can take the purchase discounts.)

Question 20 is designed to use the cloud process to establish the priority between conflicting needs in the group's job areas (such as the Receiving Inspection example about the company's need to take purchase discounts and the need to get the correct material to the floor on time). Information about both the expedite dates and the discount dates is shown on the work in process for items waiting in Receiving. A cloud can then be built using this example. Starting at the back of the cloud, the group can fill in the two potential conflicting actions: prioritize work by discount vs. prioritize work by shortage and expedite date. The group is asked to identify the need the company has that each of these two actions is designed to protect, and members of the

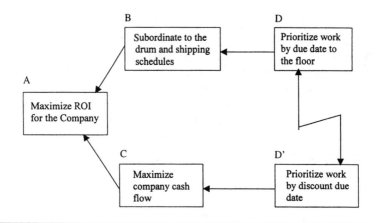

Figure 7.3. Conflict Cloud To Establish Work-Flow Priority

group examine why both of the needs contribute to the overall benefit of the company.

Using the Receiving Inspection example, the cloud would be fully defined as shown in Figure 7.3. Expose the assumptions (see Figure 7.4 for how to build clouds and expose assumptions). One assumption is that the discounts must be filed in less time than the target turn time of 2.0 days. This is a flawed assumption. The discounts must be filed in less than 5 days to allow Accounting

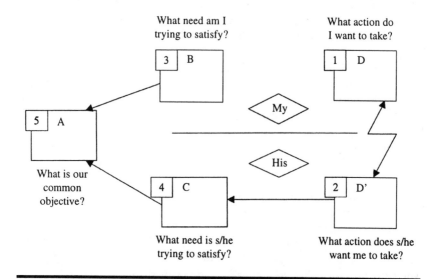

Figure 7.4. How To Construct an Action-No Action Cloud

sufficient time to process the payables and still meet the 10-day payment deadline. We can break the cloud and get both the discounts and prioritize expedites to the floor. Both needs are valid for the company, but when there is resource contention, there must be a clear priority established as to which takes precedence. This is an example of subordination. These conflicts need to be elevated to executive management to resolve the issues around the policy changes necessary to resolve the resource priority and to break the cloud. The CFO of this company changed the policy and gave due date to the floor priority over discount due date. The flawed assumption he had bought into was that missing the release date to the floor and the subsequent need to expedite the part through the shop was less expensive than missing the occasional discount.

Using the assumption between D and D' (we cannot make both the discounts and the expedite dates), the workforce suggested a solution to align the priorities by giving greater weighting to the measurement of work outcomes to expedite date misses than the discount date misses. This ensured that, when manpower was available, they still could include both necessary conditions for the company, but they set a clear priority for when there is resource contention. Their work outcomes reflected the priority, and Receiving Inspection clearly understood when and what actions to take. The win-win nature of both necessary conditions was safeguarded.

21. What is a cloud in TOC terminology?

The cloud is a logical diagram of conflict designed to force us to examine our logic around why we are insisting we must take certain actions. Examining the reason why we believe the action is necessary can cause us to come up with a breakthrough solution to our conflict. The solution is only a win if both sides of the conflict's needs are protected. Question 21 is designed to introduce the cloud "cheat sheet" (see Figure 7.4) and review what the group has just learned about resolving clouds. The blank cloud "cheat sheet" is a simple cloud template. Members of the group, with the aid of the trainer, will try to identify conflicting needs and actions in their own departments and will build clouds reflecting these conflicts.

Constructing an Action-No Action Cloud

Guidelines for Construction of a Cloud

1. Fill in block 1 by answering the question, "What action do I want to take?"
2. Fill in block 2 by answering the question, "What action does he or she want me to take?"

3. Fill in block 3 by answering the question, "What need am I trying to satisfy?" or "Why do I need to take this action?

Guidelines for Completion of the Cloud

4. Fill in block 4 by answering the question, "What need is s/he trying to satisfy?"
5. Fill in block 5 by answering the question, "What is our common objective?"
6. Raise assumptions on B-D by saying, "To [insert block 3 or B], I must [insert block 1 or D], because..."
7. Create an injection (idea) that breaks each of your assumptions (at least one for each of your assumptions).
8. Choose an injection that would work, and create a negative branch.
9. Solve the negative branch. (For a basic discussion on building negative branches and how to solve them, Goldratt's book, *It's Not Luck,* is an excellent resource.)

Conflict Cloud Solution Elements

- Break B-D.
- Do not compromise B.
- Don't forget the common objective — A.
- Accept D'.
- Break the negative branches of your injection (yourself).

Note: If this is a chronic (repetitive) conflict between you and another person, you should have the other person help you trim your negative branches.

Resolving Conflicts

The power of the cloud is self evident, as it allows the group to verbalize the conflict with which they are intimately familiar because they live in it daily. The ability to come up with a solution to what has appeared unsolvable generates instant buy-in to the process. A persistent skepticism among groups, however, exists in regard to management allowing them to change the policies and measures to accommodate their common-sense, win-win solutions. Being shown a policy change brought about by use of the cloud process (e.g., the CFO's agreement to change the policy to prioritize parts by due date to the floor vs. purchase discount date) greatly enhances the group's belief that suggested changes will be listened to and supported.

At the end of the first training session, the company has the information necessary to redesign reporting, assign work priority, and change the area measures and work outcomes to align them with subordination. The next step is to firmly entrench a cycle of continuous improvement by resolving conflicts that waste resources, confuse priorities, and arise over resource contention ("my area wants this resource but someone else wants it, such as tooling, maintenance, or MIS time or investment dollars, etc.). The area's homework in the practical use of the cloud can be accomplished by giving them an easel with blank flipcharts. The instructions are to record any action they are asked to take that is in conflict with the action they believe necessary to best subordinate the work in their area. It is important to emphasize that the other side of the conflict can be anyone — the boss, a peer, another department, or management in general (referred to as "they"). A policy, a measure, a work instruction, or simply a work practice that reflects the way things have always been done can cause conflicting actions. If action taken to support any of the these things creates a conflict with an action the employee believes is necessary to support subordination, then there is the potential for the use of a cloud and subsequent improvement. Members of the group should take the opportunity to write down such conflicts, using the template, and try to find win-win solutions. If they do not arrive at solutions to these conflicts, they should bring their clouds to the next training class or the next team meeting and ask the facilitator to help solve the clouds.

Eighty percent of the time a part spends on the floor is spent waiting. If we can get the queue out, we can improve our cycle time and increase our ability to ship on time. Can the cloud be used to find actions that would decrease the queue? What actions would a particular idea require, and what actions are currently being taken that block implementing the idea?

If an area experiences a temporary spike, other areas must subordinate to helping. If the priority is clear and visible throughout the organization, there will be no conflict around resource allocation. If, however, two areas cannot agree on the priority of resource allocation, they should check their conflict assumptions with a cloud. They should then design the reporting and visibility to direct attention to exploiting the current resource capability or elevating and increasing resource capacity to ensure on-time release of materials and sufficient buffers in front of drums and shipping. Excess capacity in non-constraint resources will vary randomly, just as strikes by "Murphy" vary randomly. The ability to use workforce idle time effectively to help areas experiencing temporary spikes (temporary insufficient sprint capacity) will be dependent on how well visibility of queue and work priority has been designed into the system. A group's action clouds can illustrate examples of possible different actions they could take when they have discovered they are endangering a buffer schedule of the drum or shipping. When should they help other areas? When must they say no? The group should be encouraged to express their concerns or questions

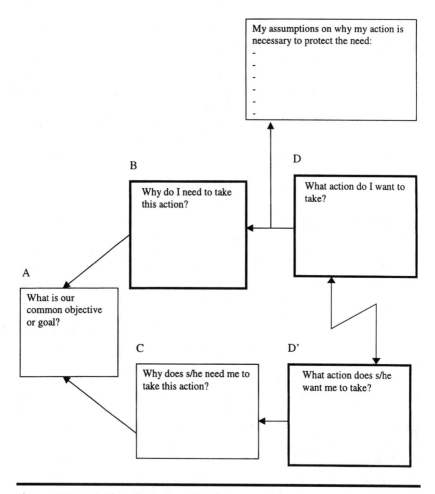

Figure 7.5. An Action-No Action Cloud

regarding what to do in the form of a cloud. The cloud forces clear verbalization of why we want to take action.

Using Figure 7.5 to verbalize a dilemma or conflict, it is only necessary for the person with the dilemma to fill in the B, D, and D' boxes. Someone fully trained in clouds can facilitate filling in the rest of the boxes.

8 | The Bridge Between Throughput and GAAP Financial Statements

hroughput accounting is essentially the same as direct costing or variable costing, as commonly defined in traditional managerial accounting textbooks (also referred to as variable contribution). Many large manufacturing companies use some form of variable contribution analysis for internal reporting; however, all U.S. firms are required by the public accounting profession as well as federal regulatory and tax authorities to use full-absorption accounting, as defined under generally accepted accounting principles (GAAP), for all external financial reporting. There is often a misconception that the company needs to maintain two sets of books for throughput accounting and GAAP reporting to co-exist. This has contributed to the reluctance to adopt throughput accounting as the primary internal format when, in truth, there is clearly no need for two sets of books or even a complicated reconciliation process.

For companies committed to maintaining variable contribution information, there are two choices available:

1. Maintain their accounting systems on a full-absorption, GAAP basis with separate calculations and analysis of variable contribution information.
2. Maintain their accounting systems on a variable contribution basis with a monthly reconciliation to GAAP.

For those companies that maintain some form of variable contribution analysis, nearly all follow option 1, which is to maintain statements on a full-absorption, GAAP basis as their primary internal format. If the only real reason for maintaining full-absorption accounting is to satisfy external requirements, doesn't it make more sense to use option 2 and perform a simple month-end reconciliation to GAAP? The clear benefit to maintaining throughput accounting as the standard internal reporting format is that it is consistent with the internal measurement information required to integrate the Theory of Constraints through all levels of the organization. This choice avoids the confusion and pitfalls associated with GAAP standard costing information and variance analysis.

From this point forward, the term "throughput accounting" will be used in lieu of the terms "direct costing" or "variable costing" (all of which are defined as selling price less truly variable costs). In theory, throughput accounting and variable costing agree on the economic definition of a variable cost: a cost that changes in a one-to-one ratio with a change in volume. In practice, a major difference is the inclusion of direct labor as a variable cost in most companies' definitions and applications of variable costing.

An in-depth explanation of the differences and definitions of product costing was presented in Chapter 4. The basic difference between throughput accounting and full-absorption accounting is the treatment of fixed manufacturing overhead expenses. Throughput accounting expenses overhead in the period the product is produced (i.e., current period expense) vs. full-absorption, which assigns overhead to the product to be carried as part of the inventory valuation until the period the product is sold (i.e., expensed as cost of sales when the product is sold). If there is no volume change between the beginning and ending inventories, then, for any period being measured, both approaches will result in identical profit or loss amounts. If a company sells everything it makes, there is no reassignment of cost from the period the product was produced to the period the product is sold.

Adoption of a throughput accounting approach requires clear understanding as to variable vs. fixed expenses. The definition of variable costs will be unique for each company's particular environment but will not include direct labor unless labor is paid based on piece rate or commission. Direct labor paid by piece rate has a proportionately direct relationship to increases or decreases in production volume. Traditional variable accounting practice has consistently considered direct labor cost to be a variable expense. In today's manufacturing environment, direct labor is typically a very small portion of the manufacturing cost structure and nearly always remains fixed in relation to short-run volume swings. Increasingly, management accounting textbooks and experts are questioning the validity of categorizing direct labor as a variable cost.

Procedure for Reconciliation of Throughput and Full-Absorption Accounting

The difference between throughput and full-absorption accounting is simply a timing difference in regard to when the manufacturing fixed costs will appear as an expense in the financial income statement. Throughput accounting values inventory with variable costs only. The difference between the ending inventory value at the end of a period is the inclusion or exclusion of a unitized fixed cost in the inventory. The process for reconciling the two methodologies can be as simple as follows:

A.

Ending inventory in units	xxx,xxx
Fixed overhead rate	× $x/unit
Dollar value of overhead in ending inventory	$xxx,xxx

Less:

B.

Beginning inventory in units	xxx,xxx
Fixed overhead rate	× $x/unit
Dollar value of overhead in beginning inventory	$xxx,xxx
Increase/(decrease) in value of overhead in inventory	$xxx,xxx

Note: If the inventory increases, then the adjustment is to increase GAAP reported net profit for the period. If the inventory decreases, then the net profit reported under GAAP is decreased.

Illustration of Throughput and Full-Absorption Financial Statement Reconciliation

The following illustration is based on an actual building-materials company (referred to here as XYZ Company) that maintained their general ledger and internal accounting systems on a throughput basis. With a relatively simple adjustment at month end, they converted to full-absorption costing for GAAP financial statement preparation. The accounting system, controls, and procedures for reconciling throughput and GAAP accounting reporting were reviewed annually and approved by a "Big 5" accounting firm retained by the company. The company was required to provide audited financial statements reflecting GAAP to its venture capital owners. The following illustration compares the transactions of the company as originally recorded using the throughput basis to the adjusted full-absorption income statement. This case uses three product lines to emphasize the different product profitability conclusions management could reach according to the two different methods of costing. The same basic reconciliation applied to the product lines in the example can be applied to programs, business segments, divisions, or any combination, depending on the complexity of the environment.

Assumptions for XYZ Company Example

1. The direct labor force is a seasoned, well-trained group. Layoffs are avoided during seasonal sales downturns. During seasonal sales peaks, the increased labor requirements are handled through a combination of overtime and contract laborers. The company considers the core direct labor cost to be fixed. For throughput accounting purposes, only material costs are defined as totally variable.

2. Total direct labor is not significant relative to sales and is therefore included with the manufacturing overhead rate for full-absorption costing.

3. The manufacturing overhead rate is calculated as total budgeted overhead costs divided by total budgeted production units.

4. The labor and overhead variance occurs whenever the actual production exceeds or is less than the budgeted production volume.

5. In the example, there is no difference between the budgeted overhead cost and the actual overhead cost. The entire variance is due to producing more product than the plan. Favorable or unfavorable variances are recognized in the period they are created as either an increase (unfavorable variance) or decrease (favorable variance) in the cost of goods sold. In the example, the cost of goods sold was reduced by $25,000 (a favorable variance) to reflect the overhead unit cost allocated to the 50,000 units of product produced over the planned production of 1,200,000.

6. The $25,000 of overhead will be carried in inventory as an asset on the balance sheet until the inventory is sold. In the period the inventory is sold, the $25,000 will become a product cost expense and decrease that future month's reported profit.

Figure 8.1 provides the inventory unit calculations, selling prices, and standard cost data for each of the three product lines for XYZ Company. (Note that in Figure 8.1, direct labor and overhead rate = annual budget for direct labor and overhead costs ÷ planned annual production volume). The data are used to calculate sales and cost of sales for the comparative financial statements based on full-absorption vs. throughput accounting in Figure 8.2, which compares the financial operating results for XYZ Company using traditional full-absorption accounting vs. throughput accounting (direct costing). Following are the three components of Figure 8.2:

XYZ Company

		Product A	Product B	Product C	Total
	Inventory:				
1	Beginning Inventory Units	40,000	18,000	35,000	93,000
2	Units Produced	625,000	214,000	411,000	1,250,000
3	Units Sold	(600,000)	(200,000)	(400,000)	(1,200,000)
4	Ending Inventory Units	65,000	32,000	46,000	143,000
5	Selling Price/Unit	$ 1.250	$ 1.920	$ 1.350	
	Standard Cost/Unit:				
6	Material	$ 0.520	$ 0.922	$ 0.473	
7	Direct Labor & Overhead *	$ 0.500	$ 0.500	$ 0.500	
8	Total Standard Cost/Unit	$ 1.020	$ 1.422	$ 0.973	
9	Labor & Overhead Absorbed (Line 2 x Line 7)	$ 312,500	$ 107,000	$ 205,500	$ 625,000
10	Actual Plant Overhead Costs				$ 600,000

Figure 8.1. Input for Financial Statement Preparation

1. *Financial reporting on a full-absorption basis* — This statement is typical of how a full-absorption statement would be prepared by product line. Each of the three products is assigned a portion of direct labor and overhead. In this illustration, the labor and overhead variance of $25,000 is allocated to each product line based on each product's percentage of unit sales volume. Note that gross profit is calculated for each product.

2. *Calculation of changes in overhead in inventory* — This schedule is necessary to bridge the full-absorption and throughput accounting financial statements. The schedule calculates the change in the value of labor and overhead in the inventory between the beginning of the period and the end of the period.

3. *Financial reporting using a throughput accounting basis* — This statement illustrates how the operating data would be reported using a throughput accounting (direct costing) format. The analysis of product line profitability is calculated only through contribution margin, the selling price less material costs (in this simple example, other potential variable costs such as freight, discounts, and commissions have been ignored). Actual overhead costs and the changes in inventory value from allocation of overhead are shown at a total company level. The total gross profit and net profit are the same under both scenarios.

Financial Reporting on Full Absorption Basis:

	Product A	Product B	Product C	Total
Sales	$ 750,000	$ 384,000	$ 540,000	$ 1,674,000
Cost of Goods Sold				
Material	$ 312,000	$ 184,320	$ 189,000	$ 685,320
Direct Labor & Overhead	$ 300,000	$ 100,000	$ 200,000	$ 600,000
Cost of Goods Sold @ Std.	$ 612,000	$ 284,320	$ 389,000	$ 1,285,320
Actual Labor/Overhead				$ 600,000
Absorbed Labor/Overhead				$ (625,000)
Labor & Overhead Variance	$ (12,500)	$ (7,000)	$ (5,500)	$ (25,000)
Total Cost of Goods Sold	$ 599,500	$ 277,320	$ 383,500	$ 1,260,320
Gross Profit	$ 150,500	$ 106,680	$ 156,500	$ 413,680
% to Sales	20.1%	27.8%	29.0%	24.7%

Calculation of Change in Overhead in Inventory:

	Product A	Product B	Product C	Total
Beginning Inventory in Units	40,000	18,000	35,000	93,000
x Overhead Rate (incl. Labor)	$ 0.50	$ 0.50	$ 0.50	
Overhead in Beginning Inventory	$ 20,000	$ 9,000	$ 17,500	$ 46,500
Ending Inventory in Units	65,000	32,000	46,000	143,000
x Overhead Rate (incl. Labor)	$ 0.50	$ 0.50	$ 0.50	
Overhead in Ending Inventory	$ 32,500	$ 16,000	$ 23,000	$ 71,500
Change in Inventory Value from Allocation of Overhead	$ 12,500	$ 7,000	$ 5,500	$ 25,000

Financial Reporting Using Throughput Accounting Basis:

	Product A	Product B	Product C	Total
Sales	$ 750,000	$ 384,000	$ 540,000	$ 1,674,000
Cost of Sales - Material Only	$ 312,000	$ 184,320	$ 189,000	$ 685,320
Contribution Margin	$ 438,000	$ 199,680	$ 351,000	$ 988,680
% to Sales	58.4%	52.0%	65.0%	59.1%
Labor & Overhead - Actual				$ 600,000
Inventory Increase of 50,000 units @ $.50 per unit fixed cost				$ (25,000)
Gross Profit				$ 413,680
% to Sales				24.7%

Figure 8.2. Comparison of Full-Absorption (GAAP) and Throughput Accounting

Different Product Cost Information, Different Strategic Decisions

The two examples, using identical input, demonstrate how a company's method of costing changes product emphasis, pricing, and performance-incentive decisions and will result in very different actions and, therefore, different future bottom-line results. Under the traditional full-absorption approach to evaluating product line profitability, the high-volume Product A has a substantially lower gross profit contribution of 20.1% vs. either Product B (27.1%) or Product C (29.5%). Based on this information, the obvious actions having the potential to improve overall profitability of the company are one or a combination of both of the following:

1. Increase the price of Product A by 7% to attain a targeted gross profit of 25%. In the current competitive marketplace, a price increase this large would result in a significant loss of volume.
2. Change the sales and marketing emphasis to the high-margin products (B and C). Through promotional pricing and sales incentives, the company may be able to shift sales from the perceived low-margin Product A to either Product B or C.

The results and conclusions drawn from product cost information based on a throughput or direct costing approach can be dramatically different from those depending upon full-absorption accounting. Using throughput accounting, Product A has a substantially higher contribution (58.4%) than Product B (52.0%). Any decision to promote Product B over Product A, as suggested by the case of using full-absorption accounting, would actually result in deterioration of the overall profitability of the company. If a one-for-one sales dollar substitution of Product B for Product A occurred at a sales rate of $100,000, the overall profitability would drop by the $6400 (58.4% – 52.0%, the sales dollar change). Neither the full-absorption nor the throughput product cost information is adequate to make strategic product-marketing decisions, as both ignore the existence of a limiting resource.

Even though the throughput or direct costing statement reflects an accurate picture of each product's contribution to fixed costs, the decision as to which product to exploit must be tied to the rate at which each consumes the constrained capacity resource. The rate of consumption of the scarce resource is the rate at which the product can generate profit. If the scarce resource limits total potential profitability, then the rate determines the total potential profit each product can add to the organization in any given period. Chapter 9 demonstrates conclusively the consequences to a company of strategic product decisions made without understanding their limiting resource.

9 Four Basic Strategic Decisions from a Theory of Constraints/ Management Accounting Standpoint

C hapter 2 briefly mentioned four basic strategic decisions that companies commonly make with standard cost information:

1. Product emphasis
2. Product pricing
3. Additions or deletions of a product
4. Capital investment and process improvement decisions

Even if a company uses direct or marginal costing to determine relevant information regarding the expected incremental cash flow, it may fail to recognize the predictable effect of a limited or constrained resource. If we define relevant information as the predicted future costs and revenues that will differ among alternatives (the definition given in Chapter 2), and all dependent systems have a limiting factor (whether internal to the organization or external), then the following is true: *Failing to recognize the effect of the limited resource guarantees that we will often choose alternatives that are less than optimal and perhaps even detrimental.* The following case illustrates all four of the strategic decisions and their impact on a company that fails to consider their organizational constraints.

When the vice president of marketing of ABC, a publicly traded company, contacted me, he described their management situation as approaching desperate — desperate enough to consider trying something new. A previous star performer, the company profit performance had been declining for five straight quarters with actual net losses experienced in two of the most recent quarters. The Board of Directors was voicing their concern, and top management was feeling significant pressure to fix the situation. The market was booming, and the company had actually put their customers on an allotment of product in an attempt to satisfy their entire customer base to some degree. The company's on-time delivery performance was deteriorating, their backlog was growing, and their cycle time had increased from 10 days to 15 days in the past year. They had recently approved a $30 million expansion that was scheduled to begin in 3 months. Much of the equipment had already been ordered. The vice president of marketing and the controller had been charged, by the Executive Committee, with the task of proposing a solution for their product-pricing and product-emphasis strategy.

The company had been an early proponent of fully absorbed, activity-based costing, and the philosophy had driven their past decisions. The controller had recently read *The Theory of Constraints and Its Implications for Management Accounting* and taken a look at their products from a contribution margin approach (selling price less truly variable costs). The new information failed to point out any major discrepancies with their past philosophy. They wanted my help to understand how to build a product-pricing model based on the information in my book. They knew they could not use the concepts in the book or relate their business to TOC without understanding how to model the information around their limited resource. I agreed to work with the company as long as the product-pricing team included the vice president of manufacturing, the plant manager, the plant cost accountant, and a plant engineer. I convinced them that they could not make good strategic product decisions without understanding where and how their constraint impacted their ability to generate revenue; to do so, manufacturing had to be part of the team. The constraint was definitely in the plant, and a cross-functional team combining the product-pricing team and operations was necessary to understand the environment and create a workable solution.

I also insisted they dedicate 2 weeks to the project. The first week would include education as to how TOC works in a manufacturing environment and mapping their current environment to find the production bottleneck. In addition, I would teach them how to use the following three day-to-day thought-process tools as the methodology to create and check the new product-pricing strategy and accomplish implementation of the solution:

1. Clouds, the logical diagrams of conflict used to examine assumptions around product pricing and product costing and to create the best solution

2. Negative branches, the effect-cause-effect logic used to check the solution for potential negative effects
3. Prerequisite trees, the time-sequenced road maps to carrying out the required steps to implement the solution successfully

Chapter 3 provided an overview of all of the day-to-day thought-process tools, and an excellent, easy-to-read guide to understanding the tools is Eli Goldratt's book *It's Not Luck.*

The first 3 days at the company were devoted to helping them understand Drum-Buffer-Rope (DBR) and mapping the manufacturing environment. Over the next 6 days, we created the solution utilizing the above three thought-process tools, checked our predicted results against historical data, and prepared a simple methodology to convey to the Executive Committee the understanding the team had gained. Briefly, we traced the history of the previous five quarters and discovered the following:

■ Five quarters previously, the company had identified high-layer-count panels (panels with 16 to 20 layers vs. panels with 4 to 8 layers) as the strategic product for the company's future. The company believed the market would gravitate to higher and more complex panels and that to remain a technology leader they would need to position themselves strongly now. The company created and began to execute a marketing plan to reposition the company as an industry leader in high-volume, high-layer-count panels vs. their niche of low-volume, low-layer-count specialty boards.

■ The product mix began to shift from low-volume, low-layer-count specialty panels (4 to 8 layers) to high-volume, high-layer-count panels. Their activity-based costing analysis supported the decision to drop the low-volume specialty boards.

■ Fewer total panels were produced and shipped.

■ Production cycle time began to increase, and the sales backlog of unshipped orders grew.

■ The high-layer-count panels had a significantly higher selling price and total sales dollars increased, but net profit began to fall.

■ A $30 million expansion to increase all production capacity, across the board, was approved.

■ The panel production process was divided into two distinct segments: (1) inner layers, which produced the individual sheets for the panels, and (2) outer layers, which fused individual sheets into panels. The more sheets a panel required, the higher the layer count of the panel. Outer layers suffered severe starvation, and idle time in outer layers increased dramatically.

■ Products were reviewed, and a product that had a very low gross profit and required outer layers only (product not dependent on inner layer

production capacity) was dropped; outer-layer excess capacity was thus cut to create cost savings.
- Profit declined for the first time to a loss position.
- A team was assigned to examine issues of product pricing and costing.

The team and I put together the following picture of the organization's current environment and proposed future environment, based on the five-step principles of TOC:

1. The current physical bottleneck was a computer quality check process, located in the first half of the plant process which was known as inner layers. The bottleneck was where the individual layers are checked for design accuracy. The individual layers or sheets are then assembled into panels in the second half of the plant process which is known as outer layers.

2. The total capacity of the bottleneck was 12,000 layers a week.

3. Although the limited resource was running three shifts, the area was not currently being exploited, and there were dedicated resources inside the constrained area that were left idle. By covering breaks and lunches and scheduling the dedicated resources full time, the production rate could be increased from 12,000 to 14,500 layers a week.

4. We created a marginal product-pricing model using contribution per time of the constraint for each of the products by layer count (4-, 8-, 12-, 16-, and 20-layer panels). I had never seen such an incredible profit swing between products per use of the scarce resource. We checked the data three times. The results were even more dramatic because of the low yield rate on 16- and 20-layer boards. The quality failure rate for the 16- and 20-layer boards was over 40%. No wonder the company had experienced declining profit. Table 9.1 shows the throughput per panel.

5. We compared the prior 4 months' product mix with the model and found it was a very accurate predictor of company-wide contribution margin and net profit. Based on using the actual monthly product mix, the model predicted the contribution margin (throughput dollars) within 3% of actual recorded financial results.

6. We used the model to project the contribution margin (throughput dollars) and profit for the next two quarters using the constraint's current production rate of 12,000 layers per week and the actual product mix booked in the backlog. The model confirmed an increasingly grim profit picture. As the mix continued to swing towards high-layer-count panels, the net profit would continue to decline dramatically.

7. We developed a pricing product matrix to show the indifference price point among the 4-, 8-,12-, 16-, and 20-layer panels. The indifference price point is the price point where the contribution margin (dollar

Table 9.1. Marginal Product-Pricing Model Using
Contribution per Time of the Constraint

			Layers		
	4	8	12	16	20
Yield	88%	74%	71%	58%	56%
Contribution per panel[a]	$135.60	$300.00	$206.10	$97.50	$91.80
Time per panel (raw)	1.53	4.60	7.67	10.73	13.80
Time per panel (yielded)	1.74	6.22	10.8	18.51	24.64
Contribution per panel per CCR minute (raw)	$88.63	$65.22	$26.87	$9.09	$6.65
Contribution per panel per CCR minute (yielded)	$77.93	$48.23	$19.08	$5.27	$3.73

[a] Selling price less raw materials.

Note: Batch size = 30; CCR = constrained capacity resource.

throughput) per minute of the constrained capacity resource for each panel is equal — the price where the profit impact is the same for 4-, 8-, 12-, 16-, and 20-layer panels. The company, from a profit stand-point, would be indifferent as to which additional unit of product was sold. This gave sales the opportunity to evaluate potential incremental business from a very different perspective, with a great deal of confidence in the predicted short-run profit impact.

8. The team proposed using the additional 2500 layers that could be generated weekly from exploiting the constrained resource in conjunction with the pricing matrix to maximize short-run profit. Using the pricing matrix, sales would target orders with the highest contribution margin (throughput dollars) per unit of the constrained capacity resource (CCR) available in the market place. For example, the price on a 4-layer panel could be reduced by 25% and still be twice as profitable as a 12-layer, 12 times more profitable than a 16-layer panel, and 16 times more profitable than a 20-layer panel.

9. We used the short-term profit improvement to gain time to align the plant resources correctly by elevating the constraint and necessary sprint capacity and to execute the long-term market strategy of being a leader in high-volume, high-layer-count panels.

10. We re-examined the marketing effort to increase the product mix of high-layer-count panels. Figure 9.1 (the cloud) was used to examine the dilemma the Executive Committee was currently stuck in and to explain how the team's plan could potentially resolve the conflict.

11. A TOC focus was used to redefine the plant expansion plan to system-atically find and elevate the constraining resources to support the

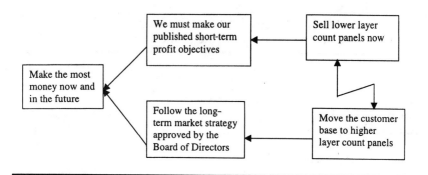

Figure 9.1. The Executive Committee's Conflict Cloud

company's long-term strategic product mix, emphasizing high-layer-count panels. This would require the company to identify where they would want to manage the bottleneck in the future and invest in a mix of resources to create the proper mix of plant resource capacity to support the high-layer-count, higher volume boards.

During a 3-hour meeting the next Friday morning, we presented our findings and the proposed solution to the Executive Committee. One of the greatest obstacles was presenting the information in such a way that we would not be cut off with endless arguments about the plan and repeated "Yeah, but... ." Because the solution slaughtered numerous sacred cows, redefined product profitability, challenged the long-term strategy, called for an immediate re-evaluation of the plant expansion, and pointed out the negative impact on net earnings of previous top management decisions, there was the very real potential of being unable to make it through the presentation. In addition, the Executive Committee had no training in TOC. This meant that every conclusion would have to be supported with logic they could easily tie to their environment.

We decided to use our logic trees (Figures 9.2 through 9.5) to create a simple bridge for the Executive Committee to show how and why the prior earnings results were tied directly to the role played by the constraining resource. We agreed I would present first, using the logic-tree format to create a common understanding and common definitions regarding the company's constraining resource. I would follow with the current Executive Committee dilemma in the format of the cloud presented in Figure 9.1. The rest of the team would present the pricing-product model built around the current constraining resource and explain how it was created and tested and its proposed use to create short-term profit maximization. Finally, the team would present their road map (the thought-process tool known as a prerequisite tree) for accomplishing the new plan and ask for approval to proceed.

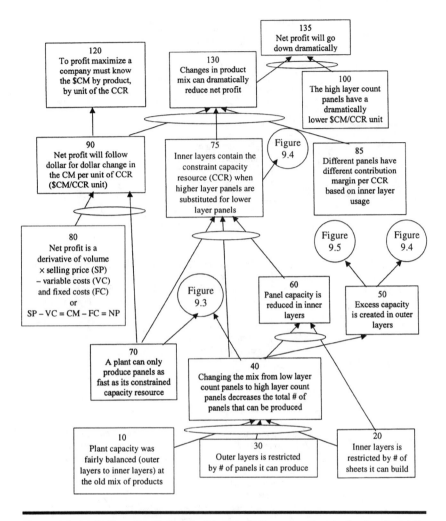

Figure 9.2. Logic Tree Predicting the Net Profit Decrease Due to the Product-Mix Shift

How To Read a Logic Tree

To read a logic tree, start with the statement at the bottom and read the tail of the arrow as "if" and the tip of the arrow as "then". If the arrow is circled to include additional arrows from other statements, then a logical "and" is indicated. Another way of stating the logical "and" is that both statements are required to cause the effect at the tip of the arrows. For example, the bottom statements 10, 30, and 20 on Figure 9.2 are read as follows: *If* our plant capacity was fairly balanced (outer layers to inner layers) at the old mix of product, *and*

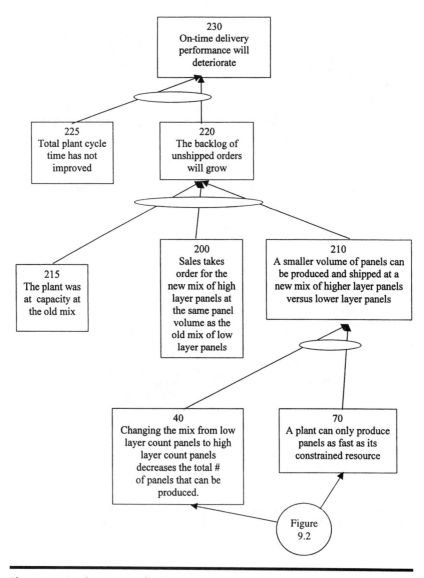

Figure 9.3. Logic Tree Predicting On-Time Delivery Performance Deterioration Due to the Product-Mix Shift

the outer layers area is restricted by the number of panels it can produce, *and* the inner layers area is restricted by the number of sheets it can build, *then* changing the mix from low-layer-count panels to high-layer-count panels decreases the total number of panels that can be produced.

The logic of having me present first was simple. I could forge ahead, challenging previous executive decisions, and stop the potential CEO and CFO

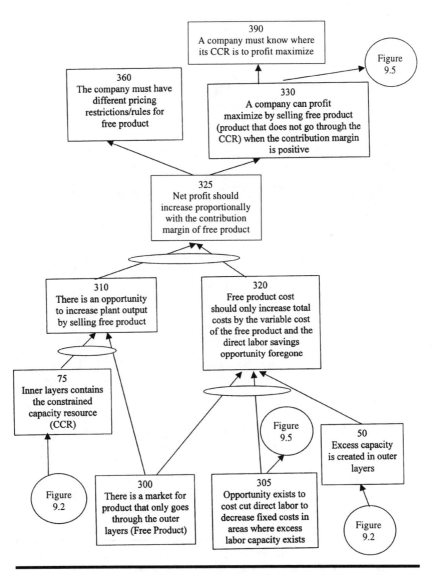

Figure 9.4. Logic Tree Predicting the Decrease in Net Profit from Deleting a "Free" Product Line

derailing with the least risk. After all, I was going home for good that night! It was a necessary precaution, and the team had predicted the CEO's reaction correctly. The CEO is a very intelligent and forceful personality and is easily bored. He also had a solid belief in the lack of worth in any consulting endeavor. He had agreed to outside help reluctantly. I got no further than reading the first three of the logical connections before he pounded the table

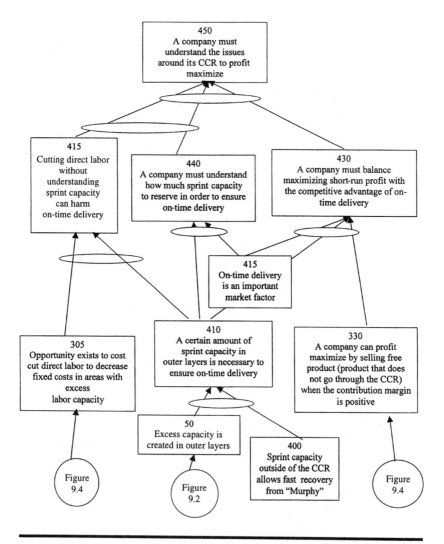

Figure 9.5. Logic Tree Predicting the Deterioration of On-Time Delivery Due to Decreasing Sprint Capacity Through Direct Labor Cuts

and said emphatically, "Forgive me, people, but what about this didn't we understand before we hired this woman?" Everyone held their breath, and all eyes were directed toward me. The team looked panic stricken.

"Thank you," I replied. "If everyone is easily understanding the connections, then you have just confirmed that your team has done an excellent job of making logical connections and common sense to describe how you got into your profit position, and we hope that explaining how to get you out will be equally clear. Stick with me for the next 30 minutes. If you are not satisfied with the outcome at the end of the presentation, I'll reduce my contract billing by half."

The team got through all of the material, and the entire Executive Committee was amazed at the simplicity and sensibility of the presentation. The entire company had been working incredibly hard for a year, and all of their actions only seemed to drive them farther into the hole. Now they understood why. The clarity gained from understanding the role of the constraining resource allowed them to see the environment without the usual confusion stemming from all of the noise inherent in any complex system. This company was, indeed, a very complex system, with over 700 direct labor employees under one roof. It is the noise in the system that stops us from understanding how to create simple solutions by managing the leverage points (the limited resources) inherent in every dependent system. As this company clearly demonstrated, the beauty of TOC lies in its ability to simplify a complex environment to the point where it can be understood, aligned, and managed. TOC creates the tool for focusing and defining the criteria for relevant information to clearly evaluate and choose the better of two alternatives.

Either you manage your constraints or they will manage you. Implementing a strategy that the current operational environment cannot support will predictably fail. The objective of the logic trees (Figures 9.2 through 9.5) was to create a common understanding and to reach agreement on common definitions regarding cost concepts, operations product flow, and the role of constraints. The trees were used to demonstrate the predictable effect on profit when a company fails to consider management of the constraining resources. This company proved to itself (and the trees clearly demonstrate) the validity of my statement at the beginning of Chapter 2. The existence of a limiting factor makes the conventional process of relevant costing or the conventional process of selecting relevant information insufficient unless the relevant costs or data are considered in light of the constraining resource.

A Synopsis of the Lessons from the Logic Trees

- The logic tree in Figure 9.2 shows the predictable effect (net profit decrease) of a product-mix shift that negatively impacts the contribution margin dollars (throughput dollars) per unit of the constraining resource.
- The logic tree in Figure 9.3 shows the predictable effect (a deterioration of on-time delivery performance) of a product-mix shift that decreases the ability of a plant to produce the total volume of panels.
- The logic tree in Figure 9.4 shows the predictable effect (a decrease in net profit) of deciding to delete a product line that created a positive incremental cash flow within the existing fixed cost structure. This tree demonstrates clearly the effect of the company's product profitability

review using fully absorbed standard cost information, which drove their subsequent decision to drop a product. The product required production resources in outer layers only and was independent of the inner-layer production capacity. The direct labor headcount in outer layers was cut to create cost savings. The cost savings (incremental cash outflow) were considerably less than the loss of contribution margin (incremental cash inflow) of the deleted product and significantly reduced the excess or sprint capacity of outer layers.

■ The logic tree in Figure 9.5 shows the predictable effect (a deterioration of on-time delivery performance) due to a significant decrease in excess or sprint capacity.

Evaluating the Cost of Setups and the Investment in Sprint Capacity at Non-Constraints

The following scenario demonstrates how to value the cost of setups and how to evaluate a focused investment in sprint capacity, investment in an area other than the constraint or drum. A common misconception regarding TOC is the belief that investment in capacity should only be at the constraining resource. This came about from the literal interpretation of Step 4 of the Theory of Constraints — invest in elevating the constraint. Investment must first be focused on ensuring there is enough sprint capacity in non-constraining resources to ensure the ability to exploit the constraining resource and the shipping due date. *The subordination step includes subordinating investment spending to the decision to be able to exploit the constraint.*

Using TOC to define relevant information creates a different set of assumptions for valuing the cost of setups than conventional cost accounting does. Setups are valued as the lost opportunity of throughput at the constrained resource, the drum. Extra setups at the drum waste capacity that cannot be regained and result in permanently lower throughput for the organization. To exploit the drums, work is batched to save unnecessary setups and maximize run time. After the drums, work orders are split into smaller transfer batches and pulled through the system prioritized by the shipping due date. The removal of the excess work in process after the drum minimizes product cycle time downstream from the drum. Areas after the drum with long setup times are only a concern if they have the potential to become bottlenecks due to the extra setup for small batches. The number of setups in areas with sufficient capacity or minimal setup time is irrelevant. Focusing on increases in sprint capacity and applying exploitation principles (see Chapter 6) at the potential bottleneck resource areas is essential to ensuring our management practice does not turn a non-bottleneck into a bottleneck.

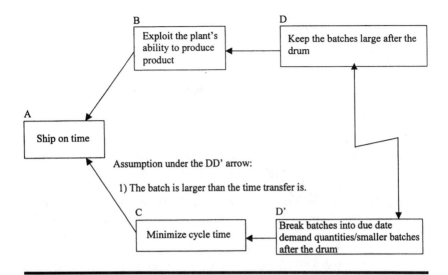

Figure 9.6. Conflict Cloud To Evaluate the Cost of Setups

The cloud is a logical diagram of conflict and the perfect tool for looking at the batch size conflict for any area in the company. Figure 9.6 is a logical diagram of the conflict around setups, defined by a client with a deeply rooted belief in the necessity of minimizing setups to save cost at all resources. In this client's environment, they had a resource with significant setup time after the drum. Like product was batched for the drum, but batches were broken into demand dates after the drum. These smaller batches and additional setups created a queue of parts at the downstream process and insufficient sprint capacity to buffer the shipping schedule to meet on-time delivery dates.

Assumptions under the B-D arrow (Figure 9.6) can be stated: To exploit the plant's ability to produce product, we must keep the batches large after the drum because:

1. Too many extra setups will turn a non-bottleneck into a bottleneck.
2. Creating a downstream bottleneck will decrease the speed of the plant to create throughput.
3. The potential bottleneck has been exploited and cannot go faster.
4. Elevating the potential bottleneck is not practical.
5. Setup reduction has already been exploited.
6. Normal queuing at the potential bottleneck will not result in the ability to batch and solve the problem.
7. We can identify the potential bottlenecks and batches can be broken after them.

Assumptions under the C-D' arrow can be stated: To minimize cycle time after the drum, we must break batches into due-date demand quantities (smaller batches after the drum) because:

1. Batches for the drum have work that is not due now.
2. Areas will use up their sprint capacity working parts early.
3. Our ability to respond to a "Murphy" (our ability to expedite) will decrease.
4. Cycle time will increase dramatically if we transfer in large batch sizes.
5. Our flexibility to respond to a "Murphy" in other areas by sending help will decrease; they are busy on nonessential work.
6. There are too many sequences between the drum and the potential bottleneck (otherwise, we could split after the potential bottleneck).
7. Sprint capacity is essential to recover from a "Murphy" and ensure shipping on time.
8. Large batches will flood all downstream areas with nonessential work.
9. Non-constraint resources work on non-drum parts and drum parts, both of which are necessary to assemble multiple final products. Cycle time will grow on all products, and we may create numerous floating bottlenecks.

The cloud is designed to take a reading of the environment and discover if the action we are proposing is based on sound assumptions. Sometimes the correct action is D, sometimes it is D', but the correct action must not jeopardize B (exploit the plant's ability to produce product) or C (minimize cycle time). In the above example, three flawed assumptions under the B-D arrow (3, 4, and 6) were exposed which allowed the plant to create a solution.

The third and fourth assumptions (regarding exploiting and elevating the resource) were challenged. The potential bottleneck was running only two shifts and had not been scrutinized using the principles of exploitation discussed in Chapter 6. Additional capacity of 15% was gained through exploitation, and adding a third shift by hiring one additional person gave the resource sufficient capacity to handle the increased setups. The sixth assumption (the batches can be broken after the potential bottleneck) was impractical because the drum was the gating sequence (the first operation) and the potential bottleneck was 70% of the way through the production process. The batch size to exploit the drum included up to a 90-day delivery date window. By maintaining the large batches until after the potential bottleneck finished processing, the majority of the operation cycle was completed, and 60% of the plant was tied up working on the wrong priority work in process. Total cycle time was 5 weeks longer if the batches were kept intact until the potential bottleneck process was completed. In short, all of the assumptions under the C-D' arrow were true, and the predicted negative effect on total cycle time of multiple products was their reality.

Note the above cloud did not include the cost of the extra setups as part of the conflict. The analysis of the cost effect of the decision, from either a TOC or a management accounting standpoint, should be based on return on investment. A comparison of the incremental cost increase (cash outflow) vs. the incremental revenue increase (cash inflow) is the only way to evaluate the alternatives. What is the return on the investment of one additional direct labor resource at the potential bottleneck? It is the increased output of the entire organization by leveraging a potential bottleneck into an area with enough sprint capacity to handle due-date demand quantity batches.

Leaving the initial batches intact until after the potential bottleneck produced a cycle time of 8 weeks. Adding a focused investment of 30% more capacity at the potential bottleneck dropped the cycle time from 8 to 3 weeks. The focused investment increased sprint capacity for the rest of the plant because setup time was not an issue at the intervening operations. By ensuring that all operations were working only on product due now, queue time at all resources was decreased. The entire throughput was still constrained by the pace of the drum, but the ability to respond to schedule disruption or an internal "Murphy" was upgraded significantly. Response time is a function of sprint capacity at non-constraints. The investment bought 5 weeks of cycle-time reduction, a significant return on investment.

10 Aligning Strategy in the Organization

Aligning strategy for any company requires addressing the issue of executive incentive plans and the conflicts inherent in attempting to align long-term and short-term profit objectives. I had the opportunity to explore how to use the Theory of Constraints concepts and tools to integrate economic value management (EVM) principles. The work revolved around using TOC to design executive incentive systems based on return on investment (ROI) both long and short term. Consistently, Goldratt's simplistic approach of tying compensation to cash flow — advocated by the throughput, inventory, and operating expense measures — has been correctly criticized for not recognizing the need for long-term vision in executive decision-making. Using direct costing for inventory valuation corrects the distortions of standard cost accounting and negates the opportunity for creating false profit through inventory manipulation but does not address the long-term vision. As companies move further into a low work-in-process and finished goods inventory environment, the distortion of traditional standard cost accounting becomes less and less an issue. The remaining hurdle is to restate financial statement profit to best align executive strategy and decision-making with both short- and long-term results.

How do you allocate resources? How do you measure performance by top management on the use of these resources? How do you pay or reward the management group for performance? Consulting firms are attempting to answer these questions using EVM to adjust standard financial accounting statements. The EVM adjustments have four major objectives and are compatible with TOC:

1. Move from an accrual basis to a cash basis to arrive at the correct timing of an expenditure — for example, accrual of bad debt reserve vs. write-off of bad debts.

2. Remove the impact of one-time events — work stoppages, gain on sale of securities.
3. Remove the effect of debt financing and become a fully equity-financed firm — tax advantage of interest expense, tax impact of interest income.
4. Move from an accounting life of an asset to an economic life — increase or decrease the asset life of machinery.

The EVM adjustments fall into two major categories:

1. Financial accounting adjustments to restate generally accepted accounting principles (GAAP) financial statements (specifics are detailed below).
2. Adjustments to account for the one-time events in the life of a company — environmental remediation, restructuring, unusual gains and losses, work stoppages, etc.

The underlying idea for EVM adjustments to GAAP financials is to isolate the issues that top management can control and to tie incentive rewards to an adjusted net profit and asset base for return on investment calculations. In theory, this will reward managers for decisions that increase real economic value and net profit regardless of the short-term impact on cash flow. The key to successfully linking EVM to the TOC is to be certain that EVM is not allowed to be driven any lower than the top-line consolidated measurement of the company. If the measures are driven any lower than the top line (division, plant, and department), an activity-based costing approach quickly emerges, and the same dysfunctional behavior associated with any standard costing allocation system occurs. The department focuses on local optima actions that compete with global plant performance actions. The traditional compromise between long term and short term is a common dilemma, and accounting has attempted to make rules (GAAP) for how to report the following issues:

1. Companies being required to record liabilities for potential damages if the likelihood of the event is probable and the amount can be reasonably estimated (bad debts, pending litigation, and deferred income taxes are examples of standard accounting reserves required under GAAP)
2. Research and development costs
3. Capitalization of intangible assets, such as software development
4. Treating leases as operating expenses vs. capital assets, usually decided based on their impact on debt-to-equity bank covenants and their impact on the ROI calculation for the company
5. Capital asset lives for depreciation purposes often being unrelated to the economic life of the assets

6. The effect of deferred tax liabilities on revenue and expense recognition and balance sheet asset-based calculations for ROI calculations

All of these rules and how they are interpreted or applied by the reporting company can have a significant effect on net profit. Even with the safeguard of external auditing to ensure a uniform approach and compliance with GAAP, companies have tremendous discretion as to how the rules are interpreted and applied inside their own organizations. This sets up an incredible dynamic, and companies become very good at "spin doctor" accounting. It is not illegal and is like everything else in accounting — usually a choice between reporting the bad news now or in the future (when, somehow, profits will be better able to hide the bad news). Sometimes actions are taken because of the "spin doctoring" opportunities that are harmful to the company in the long run; hence, the classic dilemma of the pressure for short-run profits vs. executing the long-run strategy to secure future profits. How to design executive compensation plans to discourage short-term profit maximization at the expense of long-term performance presents a very real dilemma to the executive committee of a company and its board of directors.

Working with the EVM concept inside the TOC framework could allow a company to resolve the executive compensation dilemma through the use of the conflict cloud. A conflict cloud can be applied simply to each of the above situations and individualized based on the concerns and strategic focus of both top management and their board of directors. The basic dilemma can be illustrated from two specific long-term vs. short-term conflicts created by one of my clients and stated as follows: For top management to create value now and in the future, the compensation plan must reward long-term strategic investment. To reward long-term strategic investment, the company must encourage research and development spending *now*. On the other hand, for top management to create value now and in the future, the compensation plan must reward short-term profit maximization. To reward short-term profit maximization, the company must defer discretionary spending.

Another example of the dilemma can be found in decisions regarding environmental issues: For top management to create value now and in the future, the compensation plan must reward long-term strategic investment. To reward long-term strategic investment, the company must encourage managers to act on environmental issues *now* that may adversely impact short-term operating results. On the other hand, for top management to create value now and in the future, the compensation plan must reward short-term profit maximization. To reward short-term profit maximization, the company must find the least-cost method of production and waste disposal.

By exposing the assumptions that connect each of the statements, a compensation plan can be created to reward whatever issues the company believes will have the greatest long-term strategic significance. Remember that the belief is only valid if it considers the relationship of the strategic objective to the organization's constraints. Based on the strategic thrust the company wishes managers to emphasize, a reward system can be created to reflect the long-term strategic objectives, as well as the necessary short-term profit requirements.

Recognizing the Interdependencies of Different Strategic Thrusts and the Effect on ROI

Return on Investment (ROI) = Net Profit/Investment Base

From this equation, it is easy to extrapolate the effect-cause-effect on ROI from different changes in the profit equation or the investment base. Top management chooses a set of strategic initiatives and assumes that if they are followed the outcomes of each initiative cumulatively or additionally will each have a positive effect on ROI. There are five core or basic strategic components on which all initiatives are based:

1. Initiatives designed to address inventory (usually how to reduce inventory investment)
2. Initiatives designed around quality (usually how to increase quality or control process reliability)
3. Initiatives designed around sales or market growth
4. Initiatives designed around cost reduction or control
5. Initiatives designed around improving on-time delivery of product to customers or cycle-time reduction

Implementation of the strategic initiatives crosses all departments and functions and results in management programs, policies, and measures to cause the actions at the local levels to create the outcome the strategy was designed to deliver (i.e., lower costs, lower inventory, shorter cycle time, better quality, increased sales). Figure 10.1 illustrates the concept.

If the system is a chain of dependent events, then there is a predicted effect on the system when a strategic action is taken at a local level. The effect on the entire system is dependent upon the effect of the action on the key leverage point, the system constraint. Every system has a key leverage point, the point at which the potential output of the system is defined. In fact, every department or function (vendors, design, operations, distribution, and market) has a key leverage point or constraint resource, the point at which output of the department or function is defined. The following applications for TOC are designed to address any or all functions where the constraint can reside:

Figure 10.1. Implementation of Strategic Initiatives Across the Organization

- Drum-Buffer-Rope (DBR) is the TOC production solution designed to address an operations constraint.
- Critical chain is the TOC application designed to address an engineering, design, or project management environment constraint.
- The distribution solution is the TOC application designed to address a constraint in the distribution network.
- The external constraint program is designed to address the constraint when it is external to the organization, either in the vendor network or the market.

Identifying and managing the key leverage points in each function provide focus for each department and the ability to predict the effect of strategic initiatives or actions at a local, department, and organizational level. Tying all strategy decisions to subordinate and manage every functional area's leverage point to best protect and support the exploitation of the organization's constraint is the objective of a fully integrated TOC philosophy. It is the only methodology that can consistently create alignment and resolve resource contention across the organization.

Check your intuition against what you know to be true in your own functional area of expertise. It is easy to envision a strategy or action taken to reduce inventory that could also deteriorate cycle-time performance or on-time delivery. It is also easy to envision a strategy or action to increase sales that increases inventory, cost, and cycle time by simply changing or expanding the product mix. A strategy or action to decrease cost could result in actions that have a negative impact on quality. When we weigh it all out, did we increase or decrease our ability to compete in the marketplace, and did the organization's ROI go up or down? It is not difficult to find examples of companies for which sales dollars went up, market share of their strategic product mix went up, and local cost-improvement programs were accomplished, but company net profit and ROI went down and continued to spiral down. A good example of this is the case in Chapter 9.

Often one department will implement strategic actions to correct the excess cost, quality defects, or efficiency ratings, only to move the symptoms they were experiencing to another department. For example, suppose maintenance supplies were too high, so the inventory of maintenance supplies are cut and now machine downtime is longer. New vendors were secured to provide a lower cost on raw materials, but the unreliable delivery service required increasing inventory on hand to avoid stockouts that shut down the line. Consistently, we see actions taken to implement strategy or to maximize the key performance indicators creating more dilemmas, which in turn call for more programs, policies, rules, or actions to recover from the previous program.

The Theory of Constraints creates a focal point for evaluating and prioritizing programs and implementation actions by evaluating the effect on the leverage point of each department and ultimately the organizational constraint. It is meaningless and impossible to judge the effect on the entire organization by attempting to measure all actions or programs in isolation at every local department. The mode of management becomes a series of compromises that jeopardize the ability of the system to implement any of the strategies or programs. Attend any meeting of any program implementation or weekly operations status and you will see people attempting to address and solve symptoms. *The solution is always the day's firefight, which results in lighting a fire for tomorrow's meeting.* The solution compromises some other area's need or strategic program, but the solution can be lived with until resulting problems in the compromised area become so evident that a different action must now be taken. It is a perpetual seesaw. Currently, the accounting profession is attempting to address the dilemma by using the balanced scorecard developed by Robert Kaplan. I believe that just as activity-based costing fails to consider the ramifications of a system constraint, the balanced scorecard, as currently being implemented, also ignores the implications of a scarce resource.

The reason the balanced scorecard will not solve our dilemmas is because organizations do not have a model of the environment that can predict the effect on the entire organization. They do not understand or agree as to how to best manage and prioritize the transfer of work and the allocation of resources between the functional areas. Companies may know how to negotiate purchase contracts, design the product, build the product, create a distribution network, and market the product to our customers, *but* do they know how to manage their functional support areas to best protect the leverage point inside their own function so it can subordinate and support the leverage point of the entire organization? What is the effect of how I manage my area on the area where the organizational constraint resides? What is the effect of how a strategy/action is interpreted in each function, and what are the effects on every other function

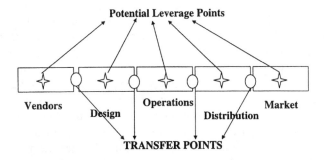

Figure 10.2. Evaluation of a Strategic Program Based on the Constraint

and the net effect on the organizational constraint? TOC provides the only possible opportunity to understand the organization as a whole.

The Theory of Constraints can be summed up simply with two words: *focus* and *leverage*. Where and how should management focus resources to leverage ROI? How is the leverage point continuously monitored and its status communicated to the rest of the organization to determine actions and priorities? If you figure out how to accomplish these things, then you have figured out how to apply TOC and you have created a continuous learning organization.

Consider Figure 10.2. The organization's constraint could exist at any one of the key leverage points. The ability to communicate and transfer work to protect or buffer the constraining function from as much disruption as possible is the mode of operation that will maximize the organization's output and therefore its ROI. TOC gives a complex organization the ability to monitor, review, and manage a few points and coordinate actions across all other functions. It also provides the mechanism to resolve conflict when two potential courses of strategic action appear to be both necessary and at odds with each other.

When evaluating strategic programs, the first step is to determine if the constraint is internal or external to the organization. The second step is to evaluate the program or strategy as to how it will affect the constraint. Will the strategy improve our ability to exploit the constraint? If it has no effect on the constraint, then why are we spending the time, effort, and money to implement it? Examples of companies choosing to follow the newest program of the moment are common, and most companies have had the unpleasant experience of being subjected to a new program every six months. Some of you have repeated the cycle over and over again, despite the lack of global results for tremendous efforts.

I have met companies with marketing constraints implementing ISO because it would be good for them but there was no demand in their market for ISO certification. I do not question the "goodness" of ISO certification, but I do question the "goodness" of the resource prioritization.

Another step is to consider if the program subordinates our efforts and investment spending to enable better exploitation of the constraining resource, function, or division. I have encountered companies implementing across-the-board cost cuts even in their plants or divisions with incredible shipment backlogs or market growth potential. The Boeing Company, in the spring of 1999, instituted a 10% across-the-board direct labor and 27% indirect labor cost cut for all divisions. Of the profit on Boeing's $56 billion in sales for 1998, 16% came from the Space and Communications division, which accounted for only 12% of the sales revenue. In addition, this division had the market opportunity to double its gross revenues every year for the next 3 years, with no real competitor on the horizon. Does a cost-cutting strategy of this magnitude (or *any* magnitude of an across-the-board cost cut) make any sense for the Space and Communications division? This cost-cutting strategy is the equivalent of killing the goose that lays the golden eggs and certainly does not subordinate to exploiting the internal constraint of one of the most profitable divisions of the company. TOC gives management as much focus to cut direct costs as it does for cost improvement programs and investment spending.

Strategy cannot be evaluated successfully without first understanding where the constraint is and the impact of the strategy on our ability to exploit and subordinate all other decisions and resources to the exploitation decision. With a focal point to monitor, predict, and check results, we can understand the potential outcomes of the strategy and which actions will achieve the best results. Without an understanding of the leverage point, we are shooting in the dark.

How Do We Get There From Here?

The first step in creating change is to gain consensus on the problem. *The management team must answer and agree to what to change.* Because most organizations are composed of functional areas, the executive team is usually made up of functional "experts" or at least people whose views of the world are very tainted by the fires they fight daily. In other words, when I put a group of executives in a room to start the process, they seldom agree on what the problem is. They all believe the problem is something or somewhere else:

- Marketing believes that the product costing too much or production's unreliable delivery performance make it impossible to get more business.
- Production points to late materials and quality problems as the cause of rework and delays that force the entire plant to expedite and work overtime.
- Purchasing points to engineering's inability to finish drawings on schedule or the constant change orders that make it impossible to place orders for purchased parts to arrive on time.

- Engineering points to marketing's unrealistic promises to the customers for either ship dates or design features and the finger-pointing cycle starts over again at marketing.

If they cannot agree on the problem, then the possibility of getting agreement on a solution or even the direction of the solution is impossible, which explains why so many different strategies and programs designed to fix the system have failed. To fix engineering, I must fix marketing, which means I must fix manufacturing, which means I must fix purchasing, which means I must fix engineering, which means... So, a solution that works in any one area must have the cooperation and buy-in of everyone in every other area, but your solution can either move your problems to me to fix or require my effort but may not solve what I perceive to be my problems. If I have a choice of working on your program and solution or my program and solution, mine will come first. In order to achieve cross-functional cooperation, it is common to find an individual assigned to at least four program improvement teams, and each one takes more time than the job the person was hired to do. The result is daily work slides and no program gets implemented successfully. Sound familiar?

The management team must be made to see and understand that what they are attempting to address are the symptoms (the fire fights) and not the core problem, and that the core problem is the cause of a significant number, if not all, of the undesirable effects they are experiencing. Intuitively, we know that fighting the core cause is more effective than fighting the symptoms and if the symptoms continue we have probably not addressed the core problem. How can we identify and agree upon the organization's weakest link and the method or solution set to address it? The TOC thinking process (TP) can be used to identify the core problem in the organization, define the solution set to overcome the core problem, and create a clear roadmap of how to implement the solution. This is how TOC breaks organizational constraints.

Unless a management team can address the following layers of resistance inherent in organizations through the use of the thought-process tools, any proposed solution, strategy, or program will have very little chance of being successfully implemented:

1. The management team must be able to gain consensus on the goals of the organization and the desired bottom-line results by which the organization is measuring its success. What is consistently blocking these bottom-line results, and what recurring problems exist in the organizational chain?

2. There must be an agreement that the identified problems are responsible for causing the lack of results. Unless these recurring problems are addressed once and for all, the organization is blocked from achieving its goal, and the management team cannot achieve the results for which

they are held accountable. What is the common cause for the existence of these problems? It is essential to identify and reach agreement on the real issue to be addressed.

3. The management team must come to a consensus on a solution that will allow the organization to overcome the common cause identified above. What are the chances of success if we stick with what we have been doing? What about the current improvement programs we have implemented so far — how do they fit? Do we scrap them, or is there something we can use in addition that will accelerate our rate of improvement? The new solution must clearly offer the potential for a real breakthrough and achieve the bottom-line results identified in the first point.

4. The management team must look at what possible new negatives or problems the solution may create. The last thing the team needs is a solution that will result in more firefighting and continued disappointing results. Unless the team has the ability to address their concerns and objections in the planning and execution phase, the implementation will break down and ultimately fail. Often the reservations of a team member are based on their knowledge of the environment. If raising the issues is discouraged and the insight of the participants ignored, not only will the solution not receive some of the team member's buy-in but there is also the very real possibility that the concern is valid and the solution has created a bigger problem.

5. The final stage must address how we are going to implement this agreed-upon good solution. The team must agree on the phases for implementation, how the plan will roll out, and who will be involved and responsible at what stages. The implementation plan must be developed with the entire team using agreed-upon milestones and checkpoints to measure performance. There must also be agreement as to the time frame for which the organization can expect to see bottom-line results.

The Theory of Constraints thinking process is the strategic tool designed to answer the three questions that are the basic components of the layers of resistance detailed above:

1. What do we change? Identify the core problem.
2. What do we change to? Define the solution.
3. How do we cause the change? Create the environment and the tools to overcome resistance to change and implement the solution.

A synopsis of the TOC thinking process is detailed in the Appendix.

Valuing Human Capital

The last subject of this book is to expose the dilemma in decisions regarding the value of human capital, a subject that we in accounting and business management have failed miserably to understand and quantify. In terms of the asset valuation of a company's worth, the worth of human capital is never considered! If it is not even considered, it is impossible to create a system to reward "good" management of it. We have failed to account for one of the company's most important assets. The dilemma could be worded as: For top management to create value now and in the future, the compensation plan must reward long-term strategic investment in human capital. To reward long-term strategic investment in human capital, the company must upgrade and retain their work force. On the other hand, for top management to create value now and in the future, the compensation plan must reward short-term profit maximization. To reward short-term profit maximization, the company must lay off any excess management/labor.

I believe the dilemma of valuing human capital and executive incentive compensation can both be addressed using TOC, but they are the subjects of an entire book unto themselves (I am currently working on both and hope to have publishable material sometime soon). Companies are trapped in two competing and what appear to be irreconcilable paradigms. The first is the trend toward the "dumbing down" of American labor vs. the concept of the empowered "knowledge" worker. On the one hand, companies search for the most inexpensive labor, hence relocation, offshore temporary work forces, and tremendous investments in front-end engineering and computer-aided manufacturing equipment to ensure that products are "easy" to make. On the other hand, companies want an empowered workforce, one that is capable of working in cross-functional teams, proficient in problem-solving techniques, and able to drive continuous improvement efforts. I believe the same hidden costs that were not quantified and were usually ignored when companies chased the least-cost unit (thus driving inventories and cycle time up) are lurking in the least-cost labor, but that is a story for another day.

Where Do We Go From Here?

The process I have been using and demonstrating throughout this book allows any company to align their actions from the bottom up and then back down again, over and over, a continuous cycle of improvement. This system has evolved because, although TOC was able to create agreement with top management on the organization's core problem, we were unable to get sustainable results that would self-perpetuate and cycle up and down throughout the organization regardless of where the constraint moved. A truly continuous cycle of improvement, across the entire organization has previously eluded most TOC implementations.

In all of the cases in this book, the total solution set included the implementation of the TOC manufacturing management tool, Drum-Buffer-Rope. The decision to implement DBR was made for one of two reasons:

1. The constraining resource is internal to the manufacturing operation, and the company uses DBR to focus and manage the constraining resource to get the most throughput and make the most money.
2. The constraining resource is the market, and DBR must be in place to gain the ability to implement a market solution. Using the TOC framework and the thought-process tools creates a powerful and repeatable methodology to tackle external constraints.

The scope of this book does not allow for an in-depth review of external constraints, but the initial results companies are experiencing are as incredible as the initial results from the DBR implementations reported earlier in *The Theory of Constraints and Its Implications for Management Accounting*. A basic description of the external-constraints process is included here in the Appendix, along with a simple and complete description of the latest generation of the strategic TP known as the "Jonah" program. The process has been dramatically improved in recent years and now deals with the communication issues that were identified earlier as being major stumbling blocks to the practical use of the process and identified above as the layers of resistance.

Not included in this book is any material or a case using the process known as Critical Chain project management, the application of TOC designed to address a bottleneck in either engineering or research and development. The same measures, work practices, and policies that are stumbling blocks for the rest of the organization must be addressed here, as well. The same processes explained in this book for resource alignment and conflict resolution are transferable to Critical Chain. The number of multi-project environments that have successfully implemented Critical Chain are relatively few but growing and need to be addressed in a case format in the future. The project management process is only 3 years old. In fact, the entire body of knowledge known as TOC is less than 15 years old and is continuing to evolve.

Appendix. Strategic Thinking Processes of the Theory of Constraints*

To achieve long-term success in an increasingly competitive environment, an organization cannot afford to rely on being in the right place at the right time. Organizations must supplement and ensure their ability to develop long-term, robust solutions for the challenges of today and tomorrow. Additionally, it has become obvious that the amount of time, money, and energy consumed and wasted to fight constant organizational fires dramatically impacts bottom-line performance and people. Combined, these two factors make it imperative that organizations capture larger and larger returns for the solutions that they employ or face continuous erosion in bottom-line performance and long-term viability.

The Strategic Thinking Processes of TOC are designed to help combat an enormous problem faced by organizations — the tendency of organizations and their management to study, construct, and implement solutions in isolation. We know that our organizations and even functional areas of responsibility are dependent systems, yet, when it comes to measuring, operating, and problem-solving within them, we continue to divide them up and segment them. By segmenting these systems, we lack the ability to see the bigger picture,

---

* By Chad Smith, currently the Managing Partner of Constraints Management Group and recognized internationally as an expert in all of the thought-process tools of the Theory of Constraints. Chad, a graduate of the Avraham Y. Goldratt Institute Academy, began his work with TOC in 1995 with the Avraham Y. Goldratt Institute, the primary developer of early TOC technology. Chad has led TOC application and implementations in a wide range of industries, including food processing, printed circuit boards, telecommunications, printing, and petroleum. Among his clients are international industrial leaders such as Intel, Imperial Oil, Siemens, and Oregon Freeze Dry, as well as smaller companies, such as Bonanza Press, Renton Coil Spring, and APEX PC Solutions.

understand the greater problem, and synchronize our efforts. Additionally, we often implement incomplete or grossly insufficient solutions that, at best, provide a temporary fix to the problem or, at worst, move and magnify the problem to another area of the organization.

The Strategic Thinking Processes are intended to provide breakthrough solutions to organizations when:

- It is not evident that a proposed logistical or technical solution is the correct or viable solution to overcome an organization's problems.
- An organization's direction is unclear to its ownership and/or management team and/or employees.
- The constraint to an organization's throughput resides in an external entity (the market or supplier base).
- An organization needs to train and properly equip a strategic-level change agent.
- A function that is particularly critical to the organization's ability to generate throughput continues to struggle.

What Does the Term "Breakthrough Solution" Really Mean?

Most people are comfortable with the simple definition of a breakthrough solution as one that addresses a very big problem or a very big need. A fundamental assumption by the Theory of Constraints is that a problem or need really represents a dilemma. There are two explanations for this assumption. First, if there is a very big need or problem, why has it not yet been addressed? The most likely answer is that in addressing it we feel we might sacrifice something critical, thus we are in a dilemma. The second explanation comes from the Accurate Sciences. Science accepts that nature seeks equilibrium or that there is no inherent conflict in nature that does not correct itself. When a conflict is observed in an experiment, it is accepted that a condition or assumption has been left out or misunderstood. Thus, in the Accurate Sciences, the definition of a problem is the appearance of conflict between two things that are both necessary and must exist. Another way to describe this is a dilemma.

Furthermore, we know that many organizations and managers get caught fighting fires on a daily basis, waging the same battles over and over again. Intuitively, we know that as long as we continue to observe and fight the same types of issues we are not addressing the real underlying problem. Why can't we make these battles go away? In an organization or area that continues to struggle with the same types of challenges or symptoms over and over again, there is often an underlying dilemma that tugs people in at least two directions at once. This dilemma often results in constant and unsatisfactory sets of compromises at all levels, producing consistently diminishing returns. It is here that the real blockage to moving the organization forward occurs.

A breakthrough solution is a solution that allows an organization or individual to break a large dilemma, removing the symptoms of it and the constraint to moving forward. This is the point where we arrive at a solution that is both simple and extremely valuable.

There are three primary processes or applications of the Theory of Constraints' thinking processes at an organization's strategic level:

1. Jonah Process
2. Breaking Organizational Constraints Process
3. External Constraints Process

All three applications share the same basic approach to the way a problem is identified, a breakthrough solution is discovered, an implementation plan is constructed, and, finally, the way that the solution and plan are sold to critical players. The following explanation is not intended to teach a reader how to apply the Strategic Thinking Processes, but only to explain what is really happening with and the logic behind each step.

The Jonah Process

The Basic Problem

In many organizations, managers are frequently unable to come up with and sell ideas and solutions that are considered from a more global perspective. It is often difficult to sort through the noise of the fires to be fought and the intense pressure to address things immediately to be able to see what organizations and managers are actually doing to themselves. Often, short-term solutions are implemented without consideration for their impact on other parts of the function or the organization. These types of solutions seldom address the real issue and often only serve to move the problem to someone else's area of responsibility. Once again, we know that as long as we continue to observe and fight the same types of issues, we are not addressing the real underlying problem.

The Jonah Process is designed to provide the individual with a systematic, repeatable process to identify a strategic underlying dilemma, break out of it, build the robust solution, construct the implementation plan, and achieve the buy-in of key collaborators. It is intended for strategic-level personnel such as organizational, divisional, and functional leaders — individuals responsible for implementing and guiding major initiatives and internal consultants and/or change agents.

The Process

There are four distinct phases to the Jonah Process:

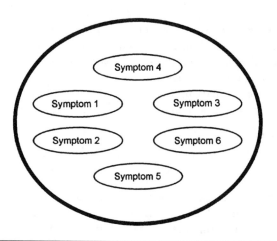

Figure A1. Subject Matter Area

1. Definition of the underlying problem
2. Definition and construction of the breakthrough solution
3. Construction of the implementation plan
4. Ensuring the buy-in of key collaborators

Phase I: Definition of the Underlying Problem

First, the individual verbalizes a clear and concise description of the subject matter to be analyzed and a list of observable and quantifiable symptoms within it (Figure A1). Second, the individual must gain an understanding of the underlying issues causing the symptoms to exist. Intuitively, we know that it is much more effective to fight the reason for the existence of fires instead of the fires themselves. Additionally, we must recognize that as long as these undesirable effects continue to return we are probably not addressing the real underlying issues. The challenge, however, has often been sorting through the noise and daily pressures of the environment to get a handle on what those underlying issues really are.

The Theory of Constraints uses a process of correlation to hypothesize about what the core, underlying struggle is. This process is called the *three-cloud technique*. It is designed to take three symptoms within the subject matter and clearly verbalize the daily struggles involved in each so that some generalities can be observed. Three symptoms are chosen so that we can have enough examples to make a starting hypothesis or correlation about what the underlying issue might be. More might be required if there is difficulty later on in the process. These daily dilemmas are the daily set of actions or compromises that

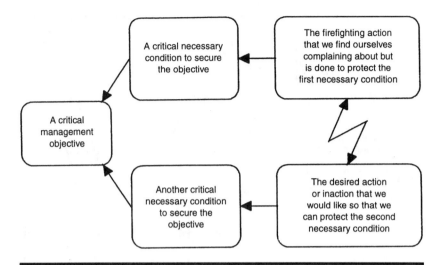

Figure A2. Firefighting Cloud

are forced upon people in response to pressure to react in some way to the symptom. The struggles are depicted in the firefighting cloud (Figure A2), which provides a logical explanation for the daily tug-of-war often associated with each symptom.

The cornerstone of the Strategic Thinking Processes is the logical diagram of conflict or dilemma known as a *conflict cloud*. The firefighting cloud is designed to take a dilemma or tug-of-war and clearly define where the struggle comes from and what critical issues surround it. When people and organizations have a conflict or dilemma, there is pressure to go in opposite directions. The firefighting cloud takes these directions, the area of the real conflict, and seeks to build backward to understand why these directions are important. Each direction is meant to achieve something more valuable, and these things, in turn, are usually required to get a much bigger objective.

The conflict cloud is read from left to right. The statements contained in the boxes at the tail of the arrow are conditions that are necessary to the statements contained in the boxes at the tip of the arrow. Notice that the cloud isolates the conflict between two statements at the end of the structure. This is the conflict area. It is important to realize that the critical necessary conditions that stem from it are not in conflict with each other. The conflict exists because we have assumed or interpreted what is the best way to secure those objectives.

Let's look at an example for which the symptom was worded something like *too much expediting*. That means that, for this particular manager or function, *too much expediting* is something that is undesirable. The action that the manager does not like to take, but feels compelled to on many occasions,

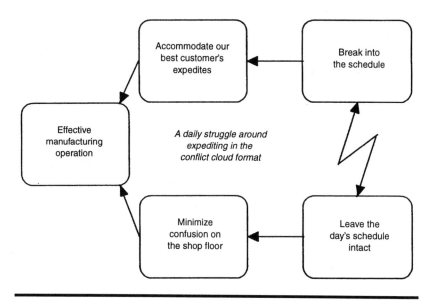

Figure A3. Firefighting Cloud Example

is *break into the schedule.* Why would people choose to do something that they really do not want to do? Simple … it is to *protect their most important customers,* and to them that is a condition critical to *being effective.* But, this action can sacrifice something critical or necessary to the effective operation of the manufacturing facility. For this particular example, *minimizing confusion on the shop floor* is absolutely critical for effective operation in this environment. That is why the manager feels compelled to *leave the schedule intact.* The firefighting cloud for this example is depicted in Figure A3.

The cloud is read in following manner to check its logic: "To have an effective manufacturing operation, we must be able to accommodate our best customer's expedites. And, to be able to meet our best customer's expedites, we must break into the schedule." The other, opposing side of the cloud is read as: "To have an effective manufacturing operation, we must minimize confusion on the shop floor. And, to minimize confusion on the shop floor, we must leave the day's schedule intact. Finally, leaving the day's schedule intact is in direct conflict with breaking into the schedule."

The real area of the conflict is not between minimizing confusion and accommodating their best customer's expedites. The conflict comes from what they have assumed or interpreted to be the way to protect their objectives through their actions. The individual now begins to gain an understanding about why past efforts to correct the environment have been ineffective. Remember, firefighting presents us with a daily set of dilemmas or conflicts. Many

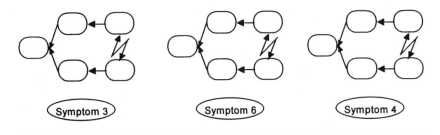

Figure A4. The Three Firefighting Clouds

times, while the actual activities of our fire fights are quite different, the reason why we feel compelled to fight the fires often stems from the protection of something that is critical — if it didn't, then we would not care about the fires. Additionally, one of the reasons why we do not want to fight these issues on a daily basis is that, in doing so, we are usually forced to make at least a moderate sacrifice of something else that is critical.

After three of these firefighting clouds are constructed (Figure A4), they can be compared to each other to look for a pattern between them. Surprisingly enough, there is almost always a discernible pattern. From this pattern, a broader, generic cloud can be constructed that depicts a larger struggle for which each particular daily struggle is simply a symptom. When we look at these day-to-day conflicts together, we often find that they stem from the protection of the same critical issues. These critical issues or needs are usually tied together by or are a derivative of a common objective or organizational goal.

The firefighting actions stemming from these critical needs can usually be generalized into one statement per need. People and organizations are consistently caught in a major dilemma or tug-of-war around protecting at least two critical issues involved in successfully completing their job or functional responsibilities — a dilemma that forces people into unsatisfactory compromises that take the form of firefighting on a daily basis. The Strategic Thinking Processes call it the *core dilemma* or *core conflict* of the subject matter (Figure A5).

Now, the individual must validate that the core dilemma, as defined, explains the existence of the original symptoms. Up to this point, there was only a hypothesis about the underlying issue developed through some basic comparisons of the circumstances that surround three of the symptoms. The individual must construct the specific cause-and-effect relationships to validate and explain in common-sense language that the core dilemma is the real problem. It is the failure to address the problem at the core dilemma that results in the constant need to reshuffle priorities and fight fires within this subject area and the consistent appearance of the symptoms. The Strategic Thinking Processes use a tool called the *current reality tree* to do this (Figure A6). The

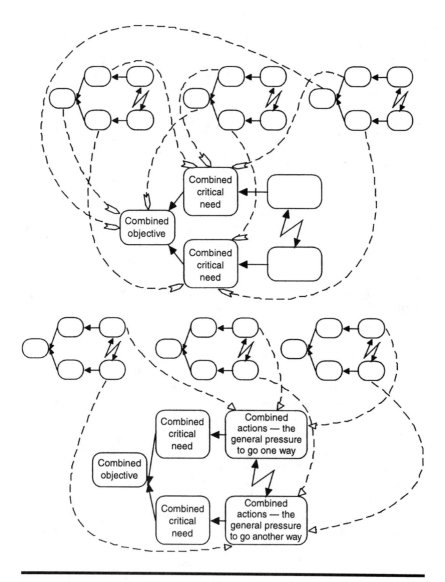

Figure A5. Deriving the Generic Dilemma

current reality tree provides a clear and common-sense picture of how the dilemma and the compromises that often surround it turn into significant and irreconcilable symptoms for the an organization.

The individual now must gain an understanding of the conditions, policies, and assumptions at the organizational level that have previously made the dilemma impossible to reconcile. Why have they not been able to address this dilemma before? Three reasons:

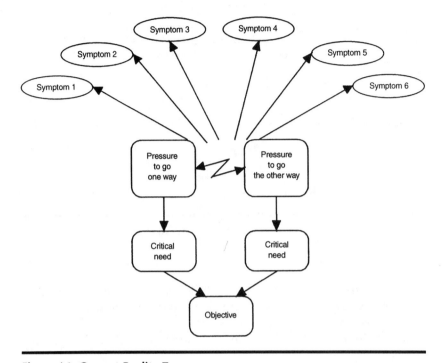

Figure A6. Current Reality Tree

1. The individual probably lacked the process, focus, and ability to see the real underlying issue or its particular magnitude. The previous steps have now taken care of this issue.

2. There are policies and measures that support both sides of the dilemma, resulting in competing pressures to act in opposite directions. It is these policies and measures that influence the way we interpret or act to protect those necessary conditions. It is critical that individuals and organizations understand the impact of this influence. Rarely are the critical needs of succeeding as an organization, individual, or function in conflict; rather, it is the way the system has been set up, via policies and measures, to protect and ensure those conditions that often lead to decisions and people being at odds with each other. The individual constructing the analysis must understand how specific policies and measures (and their corresponding interpretations) have made the core dilemma impossible to reconcile until now.

3. Finally, even if the individual understood where the problem area was in the past, they may not have been able to find a solution that was any better than the current situation. The following steps are designed to provide clarity about how to break out of the current rut and how to ensure that the solution will not be just another temporary or incomplete fix.

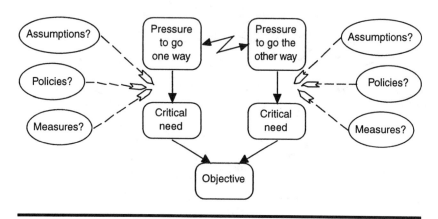

Figure A7. Challenging the Reasons for the Dilemma

The Strategic Thinking Processes call this step "surfacing" or "raising" assumptions behind the conflict. Reading the connection as before but completing the statement with the word "because" raises assumptions behind each connection or arrow. The assumptions are reasons that follow the "because" statement.

Phase II: Definition and Construction of the Solution

In Phase II, the individual must first develop an initial direction for the solution. The recognition of what keeps the dilemma in place is not enough; unless we define a direction that will allow the participant to break this core dilemma, we simply make their frustration even more intense. At this point, they are in a much better position to explore ideas that may break the dilemma because they have clearly verbalized the things that feed it. This will include exploring ideas that will be necessary to overcome or change these policies, measures, and/or assumptions about the conflict within the environment (Figure A7). The individual is also in a position, based upon their new level of clarity, to evaluate current improvement initiatives to determine if they are the appropriate things to invest time and money in. Often it is found that many current initiatives will make the conflict worse or undermine the promising new direction.

Second, the individual builds the connections between the direction of the solution or breakthrough ideas (Figure A8) and elimination of the original symptoms. A breakthrough direction hardly means a fully rounded-out solution that will yield all the desired effects that are sought. Instead, it is a kick-start or cornerstone for developing a solution set that will allow the constant and unsatisfactory compromising to stop. Supplementary ideas and specific

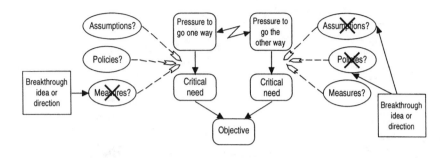

Figure A8. Injecting a Breakthrough Idea

iterations of the ideas must be tested and hooked into the solution set to build the cause-and-effect connections between the breakthrough idea and the desired outcomes in a way that ensures that no disastrous side effects will occur. This is done through a tool called the *future reality tree* (Figure A9).

The future reality tree provides the clarity and understanding that allow the individual to see exactly where the solution set came from, its real impact, and why it is critical that compromises not be made around redefining and implementing it. The supplementary components, together with the original breakthrough idea (as depicted in the future reality tree), make up the full solution set to be implemented.

Phase III: Construction of the Implementation Plan

In Phase III, an individual must first construct a detailed plan identifying the major and significant milestones necessary for implementation of the solution set. These milestones are determined from the participant's intuition about the obstacles that will be encountered in trying to put the solution in place. Included in this plan is the identification of key collaborators that are necessary for successful implementation. To accomplish this, the Strategic Thinking Processes use a tool called the *prerequisite tree* (Figure A10). This plan will allow the participant to focus the implementation efforts, ensuring that things are done in the correct order to achieve the target.

Second, the individual must identify the actions required to achieve the first few milestones that were identified above. They must carefully verbalize and explain through cause-and-effect analysis why each action must proceed in the order that they are proposing. The objective of this step is to make sure that the participants know exactly how to proceed when they leave the process and that they have the ability to verbalize clearly what they are doing and why. This will be critical in conveying clear instructions to others in the implementation phase. The tool that is used to accomplish this step is called the *transition tree.*

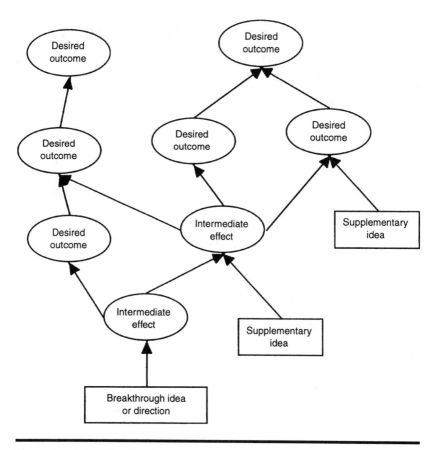

Figure A9. Future Reality Tree

Who in the organization will say no to such a carefully planned out strategy and direction? Everyone! Leaders and change agents must learn how to sell a solution, both internally and, if applicable, externally, before they can expect the solutions to be implemented as constructed and in a timely matter.

Phase IV: Ensuring the Buy-In of Key Collaborators

Phase IV addresses how to sell the solution to critical people whose collaboration is necessary. The single biggest obstacle to successfully implementing a major improvement initiative is the resistance to change from these key collaborators who must embrace the necessary changes to implement the solution. The Theory of Constraints and its Strategic Thinking Processes call this phenomenon the *layers of resistance.* It is a structured approach to understanding two critical things in achieving buy-in. First, the layers provide clarity,

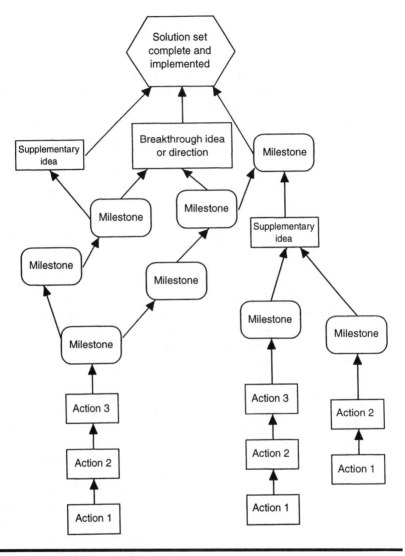

Figure A10. Prerequisite and Transition Trees

recognition, and guidance to the solution-selling process by pinpointing where particular reservations come from at all times. This awareness is crucial in limiting misunderstandings and miscommunications over the solution. Second, this approach forces someone to anticipate and prepare a structured approach to selling. Under this approach, each layer must be successfully closed before the next layer is tackled, or there will be a breakdown to achieving buy-in for the proposed change.

There are six layers of resistance:

1. *Disagreement about the nature of the problem* — Often people across an organization or function do not agree on what the real problem is. There is often finger-pointing, a call for more resources to combat many issues, or the perception that the problem is out of the control of particular areas. As long as someone disagrees about the definition of a problem, this person most likely will not buy into a solution built from that definition.

2. *Disagreement about the direction of the solution* — Even when there is agreement about the problem area, there is often disagreement about the general direction to address it effectively.

3. *Disagreement as to whether the solution will result in the desired effects that are necessary for the organization* — Often people may not be able to see all the connections between the solution and all of the ultimate positive effects. When they struggle with these connections, they have difficulty assigning real value to the solution.

4. *Disagreement that the solution has no disastrous side effects* — This is the reservation usually verbalized as, "Yes, but there are side effects." People in this layer are concerned that the solution will cause some significant negative side effects that may be as bad, if not worse, than the original symptoms.

5. *Disagreement the solution is viable in the environment* — This is the reservation expressed as, "Yes, but it will never happen here." This is very different than the one in layer four. Here, there is agreement that the solution is the right thing to do and will not result in any significant negatives, but there is still a reservation that comes from people's intuition telling them that there are too many obstacles to implement this solution effectively in their environment.

6. *Unverbalized fear* — As happens in the Army, people in this layer are afraid to yell "Charge!" because they believe that they will be the only ones coming out of the foxhole. In other words, they question their ability to help lead or guide this effort because there are too many other key people still stuck in the previous layers. People in this layer will make all the appropriate noises, even contribute to constructing the solution and plan, but will not move when it comes time to take action to implement.

The Jonah Process is designed to allow the individual to take the clarity and common sense developed in their analysis and to filter or translate it so that the key collaborators can see the need to actively contribute and push for the solution at every layer of resistance. To do this, the Strategic Thinking Processes use a robust buy-in process centered around six key sequenced stages designed to overcome the above six layers of resistance:

1. Agreement on the problem
2. Agreement on the direction of the solution
3. Agreement that the solution will yield the desired results
4. Agreement that no disastrous side effects will result
5. Agreement on the implementation requirements and the plan itself
6. Agreement by all key collaborators that they can move forward with confidence

In all stages, the individual must reconstruct and understand their analysis from the perspective of the person or group whose buy-in is needed. The analysis will incorporate language, symptoms, and desirable effects that will be familiar and important to that person or group. This new analysis will be used to construct a buy-in presentation or a basic selling strategy when a presentation is not feasible.

Stage 1: Agreement on the Problem

Too often people try to sell their idea for a strategic solution before there is agreement about what the solution actually needs to solve. If the problem is not clearly evident and agreed upon, then it will be difficult for others to understand where the solution is coming from and why it is so critical. Additionally, why should we expect others to *actively* push for our solution if we do not first take the time to show them what problem it is addressing and, most importantly, how that problem impacts them? Reaching agreement on the source of the symptoms means that it is clear to everyone where to explore avenues for a simple and valuable solution. Understanding Stage 1 means that an individual knows how to communicate the source of these symptoms — the core dilemma — to the people they are targeting for the buy-in.

Stage 2: Agreement on the Direction of the Solution

At this stage, people must begin to understand the reasons for their past inability to solve the problem effectively — why they continue to be locked in the dilemma. The need and desire to change these things are the starting point for the solution. When people understand and buy into these underlying reasons that drive the dilemma, it is much simpler to show them where the breakthrough comes from and why it makes as much sense as it does. They have a clear reference point, as well as a set of symptoms against which to judge the idea. Reaching agreement on the conditions that have locked individuals and their organization in a costly struggle as well as being able to see a promising direction for a way out of it ensure that people will be willing to explore a proposed direction further. Understanding Stage 2 means that the individual has the clarity and ability to show key people these underlying reasons and a promising way through or around them.

Stage 3: Agreement That the Solution Will Yield the Desired Results

A breakthrough idea hardly means a complete solution. Collaborators will often need help in making a clear connection between the breakthrough idea and how it and other necessary components of the solution set turn into the results that they and the organization want. If this connection can be established, there will be enormous value established through the symptoms being eliminated and the desired effects yielded for all critical parties. These desired effects will provide a source of stamina for the later stages, including execution of the implementation plan. Understanding Stage 3 means that an individual can paint the clear picture or vision of a solution, connecting the value of it to critical collaborators and the organization as a whole.

Stage 4: Agreement That No Disastrous Side Effects Will Occur

At this point, we must account for the "yes, but…" reservations. Collaborators will often raise these because their intuition tells them that a good thing might turn bad. This type of criticism should be viewed not as a burden but as a unique opportunity. Here, the collaborators' powerful intuition is used to tell us where a potential pitfall or side effect of the solution, as verbalized to this point, resides and how it might be taken care of. This step alone allows the solution to be rounded out and become more effective. More importantly, it puts their thumbprint on the solution, allowing them to gain ownership of it. What are you more willing to push for, your solution or someone else's solution? Understanding Stage 4 means that the individual can solicit these reservations and work through them so that a good solution is made better, not abandoned. By working through reservations in this way — strengthening and rounding out the solution and giving ownership to key people — layer four can be successfully closed.

Stage 5: Agreement on the Implementation Requirements and Plan

Once the definition of what must be put in place is complete, reservations will come from the feasibility of successfully accomplishing the implementation. These are reservations about whether the solution will or actually can be put into place, not about whether it is a good thing to do. Once again, these reservations are stemming from their intuition about their environment. This time, however, it is about the obstacles that they foresee in putting the solution in place, not the solution itself.

Nobody wants to be a part of an implementation project that will fail. The obstacles that people foresee are the reasons why they think the effort will fail. If these obstacles go unaddressed, you can expect people to distance themselves from the effort. Here is another opportunity. Again we must use the intuition of these people to construct the plan that is right for them, allowing them a viable route to the solution that they have already bought in to. To ignore these concerns will most likely cause the project to be significantly delayed or fail. This obviously results in massive amounts of frustration and conflict from every side. Understanding Stage 5 means the individual can solicit these obstacles, develop comfortable and sufficient milestones to overcome them, and construct a sequenced plan to synchronize the critical players' efforts. When this is complete, layer five is closed, and the key collaborators will view it as implementable.

Stage 6: Agreement by All Key Collaborators That They Can Move Forward with Confidence

Now it is up to the key collaborator to make the implementation plan happen, but how often do you have agreement within a group only to have individuals struggle to deliver on their commitments in the necessary time frame? It is up to the project leader (the change agent) to help those individuals:

- Resolve anticipated conflicts over time, resources, and priorities that will come up throughout the implementation phase.
- Break down the individual's commitments into logical, simple tactical plans.
- Verbalize and communicate clear instructions to subordinates.

Learning how to achieve Stage 6 will allow the individual to facilitate an ongoing implementation of the solution and break down an environment's unverbalized fear.

Equipped with the systematic, deliberate, and focused problem-solving approach of the Jonah Process, strategic personnel and change agents can move forward with confidence and clarity to guide their respective organizations to the next level.

Breaking Organizational Constraints Process

The Breaking Organizational Constraints Process is intended to facilitate a cross-functional management team coming to agreement on the real challenge faced by the organization and the direction it should take to overcome that challenge, as well as synchronizing its efforts to move forward in that direction.

The Basic Problem

Every member of a management team has his or her own ideas about the real problem confronting the organization and what it would take to change it. The challenge, however, is that within the group those ideas are usually very different, if not in competition with each other. Why?

Often, members of a management team tend to focus the majority of their attention on the function they are responsible for and how to improve at that spot. Far less time is devoted to solutions that consider how all the functions of the organization fit together to produce the bottom-line results that the organization needs. Why do we expect anything different as long we continue to measure functions independently and managers continue to feel that influencing and impacting other areas of the organization are beyond their effective control?

Unfortunately, the result is a management team that debates, argues, then pretends to be in polite agreement but ultimately fails to move in a strategically sound, effective, and synchronized approach. The strategic initiatives put into place are usually delayed, blocked, or killed. What are the bottom-line implications for the organization in regard to the loss of potential revenue, capital expenditures, and time associated with these failed attempts? One thing is certain — in most cases, it is a problem worth solving.

Fortunately, this focus of management team members on their own localities is still one of the necessary ingredients for successfully resolving our challenge. This focus, while usually limiting their perception about how to move the organization as a whole, means that, at the very least, they will have an incredible amount of intuition about their locality or function, and, remember, their locality or function is still an integral part of the organizational chain. In other words, they have all the pieces to the puzzle; they just need a process and/ or method to understand how it all fits together.

Obviously, just having all the intuition in the same room is not sufficient or we would have already solved the problem before now. The Breaking Organizational Constraints Process is a way to unleash and organize that intuition so that a management team can reach agreement on the problem at the organizational level (the organizational constraint) and on the direction of the solution to address it.

The Process

Management team members will and should agree on the organizational constraint only if it can, according to their intuition, explain the existence of the symptoms that they experience within their areas of responsibility. Without the ability to connect their own symptoms to the problem, the best we can hope for is their agreement that it is, indeed, *a* problem for the organization but not *the* problem. Their insistence and frustration about the group's inability to address their concerns and issues that impact them will continue. Furthermore, they will not feel compelled to assign a high priority to and work on an initiative that they feel is not a solution for them and thus not a solution for the organization.

Does One Primary Problem Really Exist for an Organization?

If an organization is a chain of dependent functions, then we know that there is some kind of interdependent relationship between these functions. Understanding and communicating these interdependencies can be difficult because, once again, our team is usually comprised of people looking almost exclusively at their own area in isolation. We must begin to help them see that the things they experience and fight on a daily basis are related to deeper causes at the organizational level.

There are three distinct phases to the Breaking Organizational Constraints Process:

1. Consensus on the Real Organizational Problem
2. Consensus on the Direction for the Organization
3. Commitment to Making it Happen

Phase I: Consensus on the Real Organizational Problem

The first step is to generate a clear, concise list of the day-to-day challenges or undesirable effects that are prevalent in the functions that each team member controls. Thus, the subject matter for each team member becomes his or her particular area of responsibility. The symptoms must be significant, not just for the function but for bottom-line implications for the organization, as well. If we can address these issues, there will be real value for that individual and the organization both. This will provide the motivation for the members of a management team to change.

There must be agreement that these undesirable effects are simply symptoms or fire fights, not the problem to be addressed. Intuitively, we know that it is much more effective to fight the reason for the existence of fires than to wage the all-too-familiar firefighting and firelighting campaigns. Additionally, we must recognize that as long as these undesirable effects continue to return, we are probably not addressing the real underlying issues.

The second step is to bring each team member to an understanding of why an effective resolution to these symptoms has not been able to be introduced within their function. The rationale here is the same as in the Jonah Process. Firefighting presents us with a daily set of dilemmas or conflicts. Many times, while the actual activity of our fire fights are quite different, the reason why we feel compelled to fight the fire tends to stem from the protection of something that is critical — if it didn't, then we would not put the fire out. Additionally, one of the reasons why we do not want to fight these issues on a daily basis is that, usually in doing so, we are forced to make at least a moderate sacrifice of something else that is critical.

As in the Jonah Process, the three-cloud technique is used by each team member. When we look at our firefighting conflicts together, we often find that they stem from the protection and sacrifice of the same critical issues. People are consistently caught in a major dilemma or tug-of-war around protecting at least two critical issues involved in successfully completing their job or functional responsibilities — a dilemma that forces people into unsatisfactory compromises in the form of fighting fires on a daily basis. Let's call it the core dilemma of a function.

The third step is to get clear agreement from the functional heads that their respective core dilemmas, as defined in the cloud technique, explain the existence of the original undesirable effects. It is the failure to address this core issue that results in the constant need to reshuffle priorities and fight fires within this area of the organization. A current reality tree can be used if people cannot make the intuitive connection between a core dilemma and the original symptoms. Most often, however, this is unnecessary.

It is not enough for an organization comprised of many different functions to identify only functional or local core dilemmas. To stop here might allow for some local gains within some of the functional areas. It might require time, money, and even cooperation from other functions to implement these local solutions, but how do we know it is the right thing to work on for the organization's bottom line? Additionally, to stop here might make the functional heads even more emphatic about the need to address their own sets of problems via their core dilemmas, rather than at the organizational level. The last thing we want to do is reinforce the idea of constructing and implementing solutions in isolation.

For the most effective use of resources and most immediate bottom-line wins, we need to find a place that addresses each function's core dilemma and, thus, all the corresponding undesirable effects that come with them. Anything less is just another potential compromise to local optimization at the expense of the whole.

The fourth step is to cause the team to realize that the struggles within their functional areas at the day-to-day level are related to each other. Remember, an organization is a chain of dependent functions that must be tied together. The struggles between functions at the organizational and strategic level are always related to each other. Conflicts between functions are a very real experience for senior management, and these conflicts often result in costly delays and compromises. These conflicts often come from competing pressures to protect, secure, or maintain at least two necessary conditions or critical needs of being a successful organization. The core dilemma for the organization must be

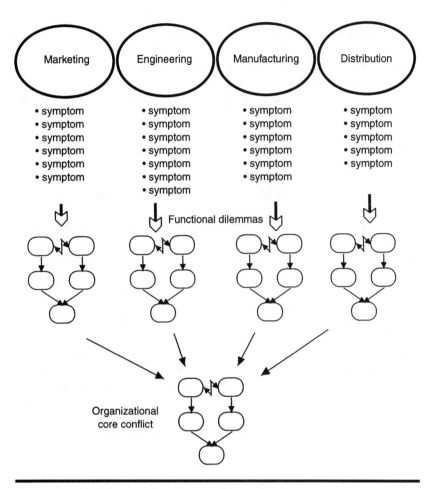

Figure A11. Deriving the Organizational Core Conflict

constructed and each member must agree that the dilemmas at the functional level are a derivative of the organization's dilemma. This is done by the same process as the three-cloud technique, but through comparison of the core dilemma clouds from each function. The outcome of this is the organizational core conflict (Figure A11).

The fifth step is to guide all of the team members toward realizing the full impact of the organizational core conflict. Here, as in the Jonah Process, the current reality tree is used to make the cause-and-effect connections from the conflict to all of the undesirable effects of the organization and each function. When all of the undesirable effects experienced within the organization are connected, the value of solving this dilemma becomes obvious. A problem defined, however, is not a problem solved.

The sixth step is to cause the team to understand why the organization is locked in this struggle. Why have they not been able to address this dilemma before? Two reasons: First, the team probably lacked the focus and ability to reach agreement on a problem of this magnitude. Steps 1 through 5 in this process have provided agreement on the problem area. Second, there are policies and measures that support both sides of the dilemma resulting in competing pressures to go in opposite directions. These policies and measures influence the way each team member interprets how to protect the necessary conditions of being a successful organization — the conditions we can no longer afford to compromise on.

It is important for the team to realize that the necessary conditions of succeeding as an organization are rarely in conflict. Rather, it is the way the system has been set up (via policies and measures) to protect and ensure those conditions that often leads to functions and people being at odds with each other. Here, as in the Jonah Process, the team must understand how specific policies and measures and their interpretations in this environment have made the organization's core dilemma impossible to reconcile until now.

Phase II: Consensus on the Direction for the Organization

The first step in this phase is to gain an understanding of what ideas or changes will be necessary to overcome or amend these policies and measures or the way they have been interpreted. The recognition of what keeps the dilemma in place is not enough. Unless we agree on a solution set that will allow the organization and the people responsible for the bottom line to break this dilemma, we simply make their frustration even more intense. This step sets the general direction of the solution.

The second step is to gain a clear understanding of which current initiatives must stay, be amended, or be abandoned. Having achieved clarity and recognition from the definitions of the problem and the direction of the solution, the team must now evaluate how the existing improvement efforts fit into the framework of the new solution. Often, many of an organization's initiatives are compromises that work against each other and have continued to fuel the dilemma. If existing improvement efforts are in conflict with the new solution, there will be a waste of time and money until steps are taken to change these initiatives or get rid of them. At this stage, however, the team has the ability to evaluate and prioritize current time and money investments against criteria for solving the organizational dilemma that the team has identified and bought in to.

The third step must produce agreement on any new or supplementary initiatives necessary to round out the solution. Once again, the clarity and focus provided by the above steps will allow the team to recognize any tactical holes in their existing definition of what must be done to secure the critical needs of the organization.

The final step in this phase is to generate consensus that the solution set (including current and new initiatives), policy revisions, and measurement changes will yield the desired effects that the organization needs for success. These effects should be quantified in terms of dollars, time, and quality of life improvements for the members of the team in order to provide the motivation to commit to making it happen. Here, as in the Jonah Process, the future reality tree can be used to paint a clear and compelling cause-and-effect picture.

Phase III: Committing to Making it Happen

The last phase establishes clear agreement on and commitment to the tactics necessary to move the organization forward. The prerequisite tree is used to establish a sequenced implementation plan that overcomes all major and significant obstacles verbalized by the team members. Through this final phase, the team members will be able to synchronize their efforts and develop a clear set of expectations. A management team taken through this process has the solution for the organization and for themselves — they are no longer blocked. Finally, the organization has the opportunity to have actions taken at the functional level support each other and the bottom line — alignment between local and global objectives with clear agreement to move forward. This is the point where the organization has the quickest and most effective utilization and return on capital and time expenditures.

External Constraints Process

The External Constraints Process is designed to address blockages in an organization's ability to generate throughput due to external factors in the supplier base or market.

The Basic Problems

Problem 1: Zero-One Game

A zero-one relationship means that if one side gets the one, then the other side gets nothing. In other words, when one side gets more, the other side gets proportionately less because the pie is limited. If, at the end of most supply chains, there are only so many dollars that the end user is willing to pay and it is up to each organization within the chain to maximize its individual profits, then there often is a struggle over profit maximization within the supply chain. Additionally, every link in a supply chain has a list of issues and challenges within that link that dramatically impact its bottom line on a daily basis, eroding profits and return on investment. Money, time, and energy have often been poured into understanding and addressing these issues, but frequently the solutions have been only temporarily effective or they are cost prohibitive. Combining these factors produces a general perception that there are more and more costs and troubles within a business or industry that has less and less, or at least limited, potential on the profit side.

What are the two most common solutions proposed in response to this perception? We can either make our problems someone else's or cut costs dramatically. Realistically, we know that costs can be cut only so far without seriously jeopardizing our organization's ability to generate the necessary throughput demanded today as well as tomorrow. Thus, for lack of any other viable option, we often see policies and efforts to transfer the costs and risks of doing business to external links (a customer or vendor) in the expectation that our bottom line will be positively effected.

All of the links in the supply chain, however, try to do this same thing to each other. Will another link simply accept additional cost and risk without trying to recover it in another way, a way that may be more harmful to an organization than the prior situation? The answer is obviously no. Organizations will seldom stand by and let their bottom line be adversely impacted without taking actions; our only hope is that they will try to recover their losses from someone other than us. Figure A12 shows the supply-chain/zero-one dilemma in the cloud format, complete with the most prevalent assumptions connecting to the conflict.

Is there really as much scarcity of improvement potential as we think, or is the scarcity a result of a self-fulfilling prophecy created by our inability to manage the linkages and interfaces between entities in a supply chain to the benefit of all? Think about all of the money, time, and energy that flow out of the chain when we have conflicting and competing policies and counter-policies between each link regarding the transfer and re-transfer of cost and risk to another (Figure A13).

What would happen if we could recapture the outflow of dollars, time, and energy spent on policies and counter-policies surrounding the transfer of cost and risk conflict? The profit available to the supply chain would certainly increase.

Problem 2: Supplier Perception of Value vs. Buyer Perception of Value

How do organizations tend to price products today? Most often we set a price based on the level of effort and cost required to be able to build the product or offer the service, plus some "fair" margin or rate of return. Buyers, however, approach acquiring the product or service based upon a different set of criteria. Their perception of value is based solely on what the product or service allows them to eliminate or achieve. Depending on circumstances:

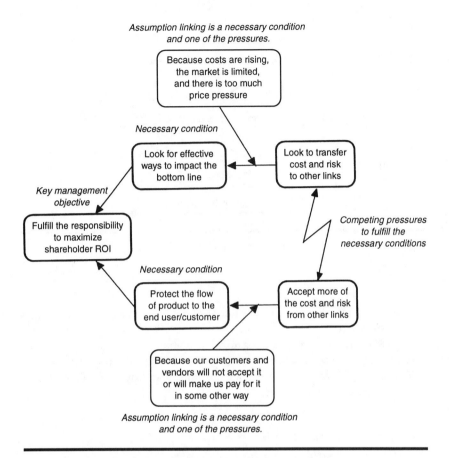

Figure A12. Supply-Chain Dilemma

- There are potential buyers that do not see enough value in the product for the set price and hence do not buy.
- There are buyers that see just enough value at the set price but are always looking for something better, often complaining, haggling, and searching for a new product or service or vendor that may be substituted at a lower price.
- There are buyers that believe the price is fair for their needs.
- There are the buyers that believe the price is a bargain for what they are able to get from the product or service.

Additionally, if, even within these categories, we know that the circumstances that factor into the value equation differ between buyers, then we know that buyers usually assign different levels of value to a product. As long as an organization does not approach the market and the selling of products and services from a buyer's perception of value, its ability to generate more throughput

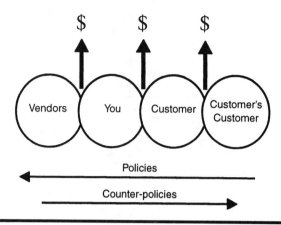

Figure A13. The Cost of Conflicting Policies

through the conveyance of greater value and/or effectively segmenting markets will be inhibited.

What would happen to an organization's ability to sell more product or services if it could consistently construct offers and pricing strategies that take into account and cater to the specific customer's and/or a specific customer segment's perception of value?

The Basic Solution: Solving Your Problems by Solving Someone Else's

If we can supplement an organization's ability to effectively and consistently solve major, previously unaddressed issues for either a customer or supplier without making troublesome compromises, then we should be able to improve that organization's ability to generate throughput dramatically. The External Constraints Process seeks to allow an organization to solve an important external entity's problems consistently and effectively so that:

1. That entity will stop passing those problems on to our organization.
2. An organization can solve its throughput problems and/or create new opportunities.
3. Price is not the primary competitive driver

There are two types of external constraint:

1. Market constraint — An organization needs more sales. If the constraint is on the market side, the objective of an offer will be to cause

the market to buy more and/or pay a higher price. An organization probably has a market constraint if they have excess capacity and/or finished goods inventory. Managers of the organization most likely feel pressure to cut or keep costs down and there is intense pressure from Sales and Marketing to lower prices and/or launch new products or services.

2. Vendor constraint — An organization needs more or a better supply of a critical raw material or service. If the constraint is in the supplier base, the objective will be to increase the availability of the resource while increasing the overall impact on both organizations' bottom lines. An organization probably has a vendor/supplier constraint if it has the sales and capacity to deliver but is having huge difficulties in getting suppliers to deliver what is needed.

Some Starting Assumptions

The External Constraints Process starts with some basic assumptions:

1. Price is not the key to breaking an external constraint to both sides' satisfaction. A company that needs to address a market constraint needs to do so in a way unrelated to lowering price. It needs to provide a mechanism (let's call it a breakthrough offer) to dramatically increase the buyer's perception of value, thus moving the buyer away from price sensitivity and removing the pressure to compete solely on price.

2. A win-lose situation usually turns into lose-lose. Telling a vendor that the problem is theirs and to deal with it is often shortsighted and counterproductive. It is also untrue. If an organization has a vendor constraint, their vendor's problems are in fact that organization's problems, because the vendor or the lack of supply of a specific raw material or service is blocking the generation of throughput.

3. The perceived value of an offering is usually derived from the amount and/or magnitude of the buyer's problems solved by that offering. We can expect that, if an offer solves a very big problem for a potential customer, the more valuable the customer should perceive that offer. As noted in the Jonah Process description earlier, it is ineffective to fight fires over and over again. It is also difficult to manage and explain more complex solutions. Asking a customer what they want and giving it to them usually only removes the issue for a short period of time, can set a dangerous precedent, and can add layers and layers of complexity via special circumstances. Furthermore, some customers may not necessarily understand their real underlying problem — that is why they have been making their problems ours. If we must have a solution that is both simple and valuable for a buyer of that solution, then we must find a place to solve as many problems as we can at once, a core dilemma.

4. There is usually an underlying dilemma feeding the existence of many problems that recur in the external entity. If these problems are really that harmful to an organization's bottom line and management team, then why have they not been effectively addressed? Many times it is because addressing the problems seems to compromise something else critical to the health of the organization. Without a way to get at the dilemma, the external entity can either choose to comply with these problems and their impact on its bottom-line performance or they can attempt to make them another entity's problems.

The Process

Phase I: Offer Selection

The proper markets/customers or supplier bases/vendors must be chosen to provide an organization with effective means to overcome its immediate external constraint. On the market side, there are many options. Offers can be constructed for existing and new products and services, new territories, and specific customers and customer segments. On the vendor side, offers usually involve a specific vendor or industry that is crucial in supplying more of the critical product or service that is scarce.

Once the selection has been made, it is essential to identify which specific link in the chain has the greatest potential to create value. The process starts with the most immediate external link and attempts to verbalize the issues or symptoms to be dealt with there. If they do not seem significant, the process continues down the chain until a link with significant issues to be addressed has been identified. This process of identification assumes that solving a more remote link's issues can actually increase the demand-pull or availability in a way that will be beneficial to the organization conveying the offer (Figure A14).

Phase II: Determine the Core Dilemma Responsible for Some or Many of the External Entity's Significant Problems

The process for determining the external entity's core dilemma is the same as the one used in the Jonah Process. There are a few things of notable difference, however. First, as in the Jonah Process, the individual must clearly verbalize the subject matter and the list of significant symptoms to be addressed. Here, however, the individual is constructing an analysis outside of their area of responsibility, authority, and intuition. To supplement that intuition, the individual must gather as much critical information about the external entity as possible. This is often done through interviews and candid conversations with

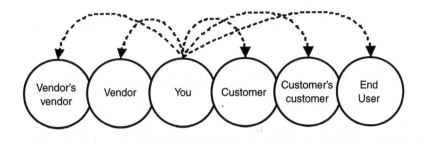

Figure A14. The Search for the Right Place To Make an Offer

people from that particular part of the industry or the specific organization to be targeted.

As in the Jonah Process, the three-cloud technique is used to identify the potential core conflict within the external entity, and the current reality tree is used to prove that hypothesis by making the solid connections to each identified symptom. Here, the individual constructing the analysis must truly play the part of an individual within that entity or industry. The core conflict that connects to the majority of the external entity's symptoms is the real problem to be solved through a breakthrough offer.

Phase III: Determine What Must Be Challenged To Address the Core Conflict

Within this phase, the individual must determine what changes must be made internally to address the core conflict of the external entity. Why should we change? Keep in mind where the constraint is and its impact on the bottom line. Additionally, if the core conflict has been truly discovered, then there is the ability to bring tremendous value to both sides.

Before we can make an offer, we must understand why the conflict has not been resolved. As in the Jonah Process, the individual must understand the assumptions, policies, and measures that contribute to the dilemma, but whose assumptions, policies, and measures should we challenge (Figure A15)? If we challenge *their* policies, measures, and assumptions and tell them to change, we will get immediate resistance from them and will probably sound like we always have when dealing with our vendors or customers.

The individual must understand what policies, measures, and assumptions that their organization or industry has in place that contribute to the dilemma. Let's look at an example from the petrochemical industry. Many of the larger companies in this industry have made a decision to have their maintenance and construction done by independent materials and services contractors. The contractors obviously can have a huge impact on the throughput of these

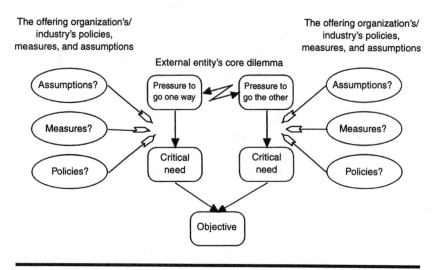

Figure A15. Challenging the Reasons Behind the External Entity's Dilemma

organizations if there are significant delays to projects and emergency responses. One of these companies decided to take a look at solving their vendors' dilemma after realizing how much was really being lost. Their vendors' core-conflict cloud and a policy from the petrochemical company that helps feed it are shown in Figure A16. Remember that this policy was put in place to protect the large petrochemical company's bottom line. Now it is hurting it because it forces the vendors into a constant set of compromises which, in turn, has a huge impact on the overall throughput from its facilities.

Things that are frequently challenged are purchasing policies, delivery policies, payment policies, EOQ policies, manufacturing scheduling policies, costing policies, inventory policies, sales incentives, new product offerings, and new product research and development.

Phase IV: Determine a Breakthrough Offer To Address the External Entity's Core Conflict

Following are the three fundamentals of a breakthrough offer:

1. The offer must resolve the core conflict and remove or significantly reduce the original set of problems or symptoms. Here, the individual must come up with a direction that will address the major factors (assumptions, policies, and measures) contributing to the existence of the external entity's core conflict. This will be the heart of the offer.

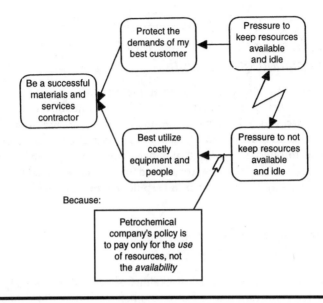

Figure A16. Example of Challenging an Offerer's Own Policies

2. The offer must provide significant and quantifiable returns for the both sides. As in the Jonah Process, the future reality tree is used to validate that this will result in significant positives and/or the negation of the original symptoms for each party. These gains should make the offer one that cannot be refused from both sides' perspectives.

3. The offer must not be easily repeatable by the competition that suffers from the same external constraint. If it can be replicated easily, we do not gain enough of a competitive advantage and are unable to distinguish ourselves from the competition. If that happens, we will be in no better position. In most cases, however, challenging the assumptions, policies, and measures within our own organization and industry ensures that the offer will not be easily repeatable because our competition does not understand the dilemma at the external entity and the need to address it. Most of the policies that are challenged were put into place to protect the industry or their organization and are difficult to get consensus around reversing. Instead, they will often interpret our actions as acts of desperation and will wait for us to shoot ourselves in the foot or claim that our circumstances are different from theirs.

Phase V: Develop an Implementation Plan Addressing the Obstacles Blocking Implementation of the Solution

An offer that cannot be refused but is not implementable is just frustrating for everyone involved. There may be many different functions and players required to successfully implement the offer, and we do not want to make promises we cannot deliver on. Here, as in the Jonah Process, the prerequisite tree is used to build a sequenced and staged plan to implement the breakthrough offer, and the transition tree is used to understand, explain, and justify the immediate actions to be taken to keep the momentum of change.

Phase VI: Learn How To Sell the Offer Internally and Externally

A win-win solution does not sell itself either externally or internally. At this point, the layers of resistance will be encountered not only when the solution is sold to the external entity but also when it is sold internally to make the necessary changes to support the offer. To get through people's resistance to change, both internally and externally, the External Constraints Process uses the same six-staged approach to achieving buy-in as the Jonah Process. The following is a brief description of how it applies to both internal and external buy-in.

Stage 1: Agreement on the Problem

Internally, we must make sure that each key collaborator (a function or person) understands that the core conflict for the external entity directly impacts them, their function, and the organization. This is a clear connection from the external party's core dilemma and symptoms to their particular area of responsibility. Externally, we must make sure that the person representing the external entity understands and connects the verbalization of the core conflict to key undesirable effects (symptoms) that they often encounter.

Stage 2: Agreement on the Direction of the Solution

Internally, we must make sure that each key collaborator (a function or person) understands that the direction allows the constant compromising and tug-of-wars to stop. Externally, we must make sure that the people representing the external entity understand that this direction will make their jobs easier by allowing the constant compromising to stop and their organization to win.

Stage 3: Agreement That the Solution Will Yield the Desired Effects

Internally, we must make sure that the key collaborators (a function or person) understand that the solution allows for the elimination of their symptoms by allowing the external entity to resolve its conflict. This is a clear connection between the solution to their own problems through the solution of the external entity's problems. Without this connection, people inside the offering organization will often feel that the organization is giving in or giving away too much because they have a frame of reference for the value it provides. Externally, we must make sure that the person representing the external entity understands that the solution will result in the elimination of the significant symptoms.

Stage 4: Agreement That No Disastrous Side Effects Will Occur

Internally, we must make sure that the significant side effects that the key collaborators (a function or person) see for themselves and the organization are taken care of. Without this, we risk having them jump ship. Externally, we must make sure that the person representing the external entity understands that their side effects have been addressed. Additionally, side effects, from our point of view, that we need their help with must be worked through. The assumption is that at this point they will be willing to cooperate in helping resolve these issues because the offering is very promising from their perspective.

Stage 5: Agreement on the Implementation Requirements and Plan

Internally, we must make sure that the obstacles that the key collaborators (a function or person) see for the implementation are taken care of. Externally, we must make sure that people representing the external entity understand that their obstacles for the implementation will be addressed. Additionally, obstacles, from our point of view, that we need their help with must be worked through. Once again, the assumption is that they will be willing to cooperate to resolve these issues if the previous layers have been successfully addressed.

Stage 6: Agreement by Key Collaborators That They Can Move Forward with Confidence

Internally, we must make sure that the key collaborators (a function or person) have the continual support of the internal change agent to work through things as they arise. Externally, we must make sure that the people representing the external entity understand that our organization is committed and willing to support their efforts, if necessary. This often includes things such as presentations to their bosses or senior management, thus removing their burden of selling the solution to their internal structure.

Summary

The Strategic Thinking Processes of TOC can be applied in different forms, depending on the strategic needs of an organization. Through a systematic and deliberate process of problem-solving, the Strategic Thinking Processes are designed to address the non-physical constraints that hold organizations back. When combined, the logistical applications and day-to-day thinking processes of TOC give an organization the ability to effectively tie its actions at all levels together, accelerate the pace of improvement, and adapt to changes in the environment.

Index

W

work-in-process inventory, 6, 24, 32, 36,
    47, 64, 69, 80, 87, 93, 131

Y

yellow zone, 66

Z

zero-one game, 165–166